The Method of Multiple Hypotheses

This book illustrates the method of multiple hypotheses with detailed examples and describes the limitations facing all methods (including the method of multiple hypotheses) as the means for constructing knowledge about nature.

Author Charles Reichardt explains the method of multiple hypotheses using a range of real-world applications involving the causes of crime, traffic fatalities, and home field advantage in sports. The book describes the benefits of utilizing multiple hypotheses and the inherent limitations within which all methods must operate because all conclusions about nature must remain tentative and forever subject to revision. Nonetheless, the book reveals how the method of multiple hypotheses can produce strong inferences even in the face of the inevitable uncertainties of knowledge. The author also explicates some of the most foundational ideas in the philosophy of science including the notions of the underdetermination of theory by data, the Duhem-Quine thesis, and the theory-ladenness of observation.

This book will be important reading for advanced undergraduates, graduates, and professional researchers across the social, behavioral, and natural sciences wanting to understand this method and how to apply it to their field of interest.

Charles S. Reichardt is Professor of Psychology at the University of Denver and a fellow of the Association for Psychological Science. He is a recipient of the President's Prize from the Evaluation Research Society and the Tanaka Award from the Society of Multivariate Experimental Psychology. He is the author of *Quasi-Experimentation: A Guide to Design and Analysis.*

The Method of Multiple Hypotheses

A Guide for Professional and Academic Researchers

Charles S. Reichardt

Routledge
Taylor & Francis Group
NEW YORK AND LONDON

First published 2022
by Routledge
605 Third Avenue, New York, NY 10158

and by Routledge
2 Park Square, Milton Park, Abingdon, Oxon OX14 4RN

Routledge is an imprint of the Taylor & Francis Group, an informa business

Library of Congress Cataloging-in-Publication Data
A catalog record for this title has been requested

ISBN: 978-1-032-05623-4 (hbk)
ISBN: 978-1-032-05460-5 (pbk)
ISBN: 978-1-003-19841-3 (ebk)

DOI: 10.4324/9781003198413

Typeset in Bembo
by Taylor & Francis Books

To BJU, DTC, and TDC for teaching me the value of alternative hypotheses. To ALS for encouraging me to always consider alternative hypotheses.

Contents

Figures

Acknowledgments

My thinking about alternative hypotheses was inspired and enlightened by the writings and teachings of Benton J. Underwood, Donald T. Campbell, and Thomas D. Cook. In addition to my intellectual debts to them, I owe sincere thanks to those who read and commented on drafts of this book. These wonderful and insightful souls include Damon Abraham, Mike Edwards, Chris Gunderson, C. Deborah Laughton, Mel Mark, George Potts, Scott Stanley, and Tim Sweeny. I also thank Anne Strobridge for her never ending support and encouragement.

Chapter 1

Introduction

Naïve realism is the belief that evidence speaks for itself. The notion is that if you simply open your eyes, you can see reality as it truly is. What you see is what you get. Such sentiments provide a highly appealing and, often times, a highly persuasive perspective. For example, I can tell there is a computer in front of me merely by looking, can't I? Certainly in this instance, it is highly unlikely that my eyes deceive me. But there is ample reason to believe our senses and the empirical evidence they produce can, and often does, mislead us. Visual illusions are striking examples. And there are innumerable instances where people, including scientists, have entertained false beliefs because empirical evidence was misinterpreted. For example, the fact the earth revolves around the sun appears to be directly contradicted by our senses, which is why a stable earth was taken for granted for such a large proportion of human existence. Or consider that chemists used to believe evidence favored the theory that heat was derived from a substance (i.e., the caloric theory of heat) rather than molecular motion (i.e., the kinetic theory of heat), and the persuasiveness of the caloric theory perhaps explains the pervasiveness of the use of the name *calories* as the units of measurement even today (Goldstein & Goldstein, 1984). Newton's laws of mechanics were taken as gospel for two centuries before they were replaced by Einstein's theories of relativity. And many sinister beliefs, such as in the existence of witches, were thought to be based on good evidence and thereby used to justify appalling cruelty. The point is that, to make sense of the world, our perceptual experiences must be interpreted and they can be, and often have been, interpreted incorrectly.

My mission is to explain how we can make sense of our sense experiences to know what is true rather than what might seem to be true. I restrict my focus to knowing what is true about nature. I'm not interested in philosophical questions about what is ethical, what is beautiful, or what is God. I'm concerned only with knowledge about what exists in the natural world. This is the realm of science. I propose to explicate the method by which science obtains knowledge because science is the best method for knowing nature. That is, I propose to explicate the scientific method. But what I propose is not how the scientific method is often described. The hypothetico-deductive method is often described as the scientific method. I reject this description. The real scientific method is the method of multiple hypotheses.

DOI: 10.4324/9781003198413-1

To summarize the arguments in my book ever so briefly, I claim the scientific way of knowing (the method of multiple hypotheses) requires two conditions. To provide a context, suppose we are interested in knowing whether hypothesis X about reality is true. The two conditions that must be met for a belief in hypothesis X to be well justified are that (a) empirical evidence, even though fallible, is in good agreement with hypothesis X and (b) empirical evidence is not in as good agreement with alternatives to hypothesis X as with hypothesis X. The first condition is obvious: If we are to be well justified in believing hypothesis X about reality, empirical evidence should be in good agreement with hypothesis X. Descriptions of the scientific method usually include reference to this first condition for warranting a belief in hypothesis X. The second condition specifies that justifying belief in hypothesis X requires putting alternative hypotheses into competition with hypothesis X to insure hypothesis X agrees with evidence better than the alternatives. This second condition is often given short shrift in descriptions of the scientific method. As a result, this second condition needs to be emphasized. Providing such emphasis is a primary purpose of this volume. The name I give to the method of justifying the belief in a hypothesis, the method of multiple hypotheses, emphasizes the second condition. I claim the method of multiple hypotheses is the best way to produce justified inferences about nature.

I am not alone in my emphasis on identifying multiple hypotheses and eliminating those hypotheses that don't agree with the data as the best route to obtaining knowledge. Consider the work of five others.

First, in 1890, the geologist Thomas Chamberlin published an article in *Science*, which was entitled "The method of multiple working hypotheses" and which, because of its importance, was reprinted in *Science* seventy-five years later (Chamberlin, 1890/1965). Chamberlin proposed that scientists (as well as thinkers in general) are well advised to hold multiple hypotheses in mind at any one time rather than focusing on just a single hypothesis. One advantage of the multiple hypotheses approach arises because, when only a single hypothesis is being investigated, researchers can become emotionally attached to that hypothesis and thereby become biased in their investigations. More prosaically, Chamberlin (1965) likens the approval of one's own theoretical explanation to the acceptance of one's child. That is, researchers love a theory of their own creation much as they love their own human offspring. Affection only grows as the theory develops and, like the affection for a child, the affection for a theory is not impartial. Try as they might to keep their belief in their own theories tentative and unprejudiced, researchers are unable to keep their hopes and dreams for the success of their theories in check. In particular, without being able to maintain disinterest in their work, researchers' evaluation of the evidence collected to test their theories no longer remains unbiased. As Chamberlin (1965) explains:

> The mind lingers with pleasure upon the facts that fall happily into the embrace of the theory, and feels a natural coldness toward those that seem

> refractory. Instinctively there is a special searching out of phenomena that support it, for the mind is led by its desires.
>
> (p. 755)

Although Chamberlin does not use the term, he is describing the effects of confirmation bias. When a single hypothesis is kept in mind, data are sought that support the hypothesis more than data that oppose the hypothesis. Data are either consciously or unconsciously shaped to fit the hypothesis. The researcher challenges the veracity of data that do not fit the hypothesis more than the veracity of data that do fit. It is such tendencies that lead to biases in the inferences that are drawn about the state of reality. Chamberlin's (1965) recommended way to avoid affection for a single hypothesis and thereby avoid confirmation biases is to keep multiple hypotheses in mind. Chamberlin (1965) proposes other benefits of pursuing multiple hypotheses as well. With multiple, rather than single, hypotheses, the researcher is more likely to develop appropriately complex hypotheses, more likely to discover data that discriminate among hypotheses, and more likely to draw inferences based on adequate evidence.

Second, in 1964, the physicist John Platt published an article in *Science* entitled "Strong Inference," which became widely popular, garnering thousands of citations. Platt references and elaborates upon Chamberlin's work. The main thesis of Platt's article is that the most profound advances in science are achieved by creating alternative hypotheses as explanations for a given phenomenon, carrying out experiments to distinguish among the hypotheses, and repeating this process so the number of alternative hypotheses is winnowed down. According to Platt (1964), the means to the best and quickest results is "to set down explicitly at each step just what the question is, and what all the alternatives are, and then to set up crucial experiments to try to disprove some" (p. 352). Platt calls his proposed method for rapid progress in science *strong inference*. I prefer to think of his method as the method of multiple hypotheses and that strong inference is the result of that method, when the method is rigorously applied.

Third, Donald Campbell (1957) introduced the seminal notions of threats to internal and external validity, which are alternative hypotheses (or rival explanations) for a conclusion about cause and effect. Campbell proposed that conclusions about cause and effect must take account of the alternative hypotheses that he and his colleagues have painstakingly enumerated (Campbell & Stanley, 1966; Cook & Campbell, 1979; Shadish, Cook, & Campbell, 2002). Firm conclusions about the effects of a specific cause can be drawn only by identifying and then eliminating the multiple hypotheses that threaten correct inferences about causality. The value of examining multiple hypotheses and multiple data sources has also been established under the rubric of critical multiplism (Cook, 1985; Shadish, 1993).

Fourth, Carl Sagan (1995) succinctly summarized my argument when he wrote:

> We invent, if we can, a rich array of possible explanations and systematically confront each explanation with the facts. … If there's something to be

> explained, think of all the different ways in which it *could* be explained. Then think of tests by which you might systematically disprove each of the alternatives.
>
> (pp. 209–210, emphasis in original)

And fifth, Johnson, Russo and Schoonenboom (2019) were even more succinct: "one always needs to rule out alternative explanations when making a claim" (p. 157).

This volume builds upon these prior works by further elaborating the method of multiple hypotheses. In the ensuing chapters, I explicate the logic of the method of multiple hypotheses and provide three, in-depth illustrations of the method. I explain the benefits of the method of multiple hypotheses by contrasting it with the hypothetico-deductive method, which is the classic and far more widely cited method for warranting claims about nature. I also explain why no method (including the method of multiple hypotheses) can either prove or disprove a hypothesis about nature and that researchers must accept this inevitable fate of uncertainty. I nonetheless justify the use of the method of multiple hypotheses in the face of the fallibility of scientific knowledge claims.

The method of multiple hypotheses applies to all sciences and not just the so-called natural sciences such as chemistry and physics. All the sciences, including the social and behavioral sciences such as anthropology, economics, education, political science, psychology, and sociology, are based at their best upon the method of multiple hypotheses just as are the natural sciences (Carey, 2004; Kaplan, 1964). Hence the audience for this volume is intended to be those interested in any of the scientific endeavors.

Although identifying and assessing alternative hypotheses lies at the heart of the scientific way of knowing, identifying and assessing alternative hypotheses is not unique to science. Anyone interested in knowing reality, which includes police detectives, doctors, and auto mechanics among many others, are well served by identifying and assessing alternative hypotheses and putting them into competition. Putting alternative hypotheses into competition is also a critical component of critical thinking generally (Ennis, 1987). Hence the reach of this book is intended to go beyond science. This book is intended to serve all those who wish to discern reality well and to think well. Science, along with its method of multiple hypotheses, is the best way "humanity has so far devised for effectively directed reflection" (Dewey, 1966, p. 189).

There is nothing mystical or magical about science or the method of multiple hypotheses. They are straightforward and perfectly logical. They are based on common sense and differ from common sense only in being more codified and refined. As Bronowski (1978) explained, the scientific method is "the method of all human enquiry, which differs at last only in this, that it is explicit and systematic" (p. 121). Or as Phillips (1992a) noted, "[S]cience embodies exactly the same types of fallible reasoning as is found elsewhere—it is just that scientists do, a little more self-consciously and in a more controlled way, what all effective thinkers do" (p. 50). Effective thinkers need to guard against mistaken beliefs. Science and the method of multiple hypotheses are refinements of common sense as a means to keep us from fooling ourselves with mistaken beliefs.

Science evolved in response to naïve realism and other faulty beliefs as a means to interpret empirical data as accurately as possible. Although science can still get things wrong, as myriad examples attest, there is still a widespread and justifiable belief that science is the best means we have for understanding reality correctly. And in spite of its many mistakes, science has been remarkably successful in providing a useful understanding of the world.

As a result of science's success in understanding the world, to call something *scientific* usually accords it a certain degree of respect. For example, if the effectiveness of a commercial product is said to be established by scientific test, it is meant to imply that claims of the product's effectiveness are highly credible. That a theory is assessed scientifically is meant to imply the test of the theory is rigorous and unbiased, and hence the results of the test are of high quality. And scientific advances are often accorded high status because they lead to the development of such things as life-saving technologies, even though some scientific advances also lead to things such as weapons of mass destruction.

It is the methods of science that make scientific results so reliable and noteworthy. The question I am asking in this volume is what is the method by which such reliability and noteworthiness are produced? What is the scientific way of knowing? The answer is the method of multiple hypotheses.

Chapter 2

The Hypothetico-Deductive Method

The central task of science is to come to understand reality. The purpose of this book is to describe the best means by which science justifies beliefs about reality.

I am going to start my treatise by briefly describing, in the present chapter, the hypothetico-deductive method as a means of justifying one's beliefs about reality. But, dear reader, please note that although I start with the hypothetico-deductive method I do not endorse it. What I recommend as the means of justifying one's beliefs, the method of multiple hypotheses, is presented in the chapter after this one. Nonetheless, the hypothetico-deductive method is very commonly discussed and very widely recommended by others and so provides a necessary contrast to the method of multiple hypotheses. Because the hypothetico-deductive method is simpler than the method of multiple hypotheses, I present the hypothetico-deductive method first.

The Hypothetico-Deductive (H-D) Method as the Received View

If you google *scientific method* on the internet, you will find any number of references and websites that present the scientific method as a series of steps. You will also frequently find such series of steps in textbooks. For example, the steps are often presented as the scientific method or as the accepted research process in introductory textbooks in psychology (Coon & Mitterer, 2016; Feldman, 2011; Grison, Heatherton, Gazzaniga, 2017; Weiten, 2013) and sociology (Giddens, Duneier, Applebaum, & Carr, 2016; OpenStax, 2019). The steps are also often presented as the scientific method or as the accepted research process in textbooks on research methods (Adams & Lawrence, 2019; Marder, 2011; Privitera & Ahlgrim-Delzell, 2019). Perhaps the steps are what you have been taught is the scientific method throughout your schooling, as they have been taught for generations (Russell, 1931).

The steps in this purported scientific method are often labeled the hypothetico-deductive (H-D) method. The number of steps as well as the exact specification and degree of complexity of the H-D method varies. But the heart of the H-D method, as it is most often presented, consists of the following foundational steps proceeding one after the other:

DOI: 10.4324/9781003198413-2

1 Observe a phenomenon.
2 Formulate a hypothesis to explain the phenomenon.
3 Derive consequences or implications of the hypothesis.
4 Collect data to assess the consequences or implications of the hypothesis.
5 Conclude the hypothesis is either confirmed or rejected based on the results of the assessment.

Russell (1931) simplified the H-D process into three stages:

> [T]he first consists of observing the significant facts; the second in arriving at a hypothesis, which, if it is true would account for these facts; the third is deducing from this hypothesis consequences which can be tested by observation. If the consequences are verified, the hypothesis is provisionally accepted as true, although it will usually require modification later on as a result of the discovery of further facts.
>
> (p. 57)

Using even fewer words, a description of the H-D method is the following: A hypothesis is proposed, implications of the hypothesis are deduced, data are collected to assess the implications, and conclusions are drawn. The name *hypothetico-deductive* focuses on the two steps of formulating a hypothesis and deducing empirical consequences or implications, which are then assessed.

The basic steps presented above can be embellished with additional steps. For example, a literature review might be added toward the beginning of the process. Or steps involving the communication of the results of the study along with a replication of the results are sometimes added at the end. And sometimes intermediate steps are added to make clear that any study being conducted must first be designed and the data that are collected must be analyzed and interpreted before conclusions can be drawn. In addition, disagreements can arise, such as about the order of the steps. For example, contrary to the order I have given above, Popper (1965) argued that initial observations come only after a hypothesis is specified because observations must be guided by a hypothesis, otherwise a researcher would not know what to observe. In any case, and in spite of differences, the rudiments of the purported research process remain much the same across different depictions of the H-D method.

The results of the test of the hypothesis specified in the H-D method are said to either support or refute that hypothesis. If the results of the test support the hypothesis, the hypothesis is accepted as if it is correct. As Carey (2004) explained the method: "If we get the results we have predicted, we have good reasons to believe our explanation is right" (p. 4). With positive outcomes such as that, the H-D method is sometimes depicted as coming to an end after researchers take steps such as communicating the results of the investigation. In other depictions, the H-D method is said to loop back on itself in an iterative fashion whereby additional tests of the hypothesis are conducted or new phenomena are investigated. Or when the results of a test disconfirm the hypothesis under study, the original hypothesis might be either modified or rejected and replaced. In this latter case, the H-D method is again depicted as iteratively looping back on itself wherein the process is repeated with the derivation of consequences or implications of the new hypothesis, tests of the consequences, drawing of conclusions, and so on.

In any case, the H-D method focuses on only a single hypothesis at a time. Little, if anything, is said about comparing alternative hypotheses. And even if more than a single hypothesis is considered (when the H-D process is said to iteratively loop back on itself), multiple hypotheses are still considered only one at a time in isolation. In contrast, the method of multiple hypotheses (MH) directly compares alternative hypotheses. As a result, the MH method is superior to the H-D methods as a means of belief justification. The MH method is superior to the H-D method precisely because it acknowledges the critical role played by the direct comparison of alternative hypotheses. The MH method is the ultimate bedrock upon which the justification of beliefs about reality should rest. Because it focuses on a single hypothesis in isolation, the H-D method is not an adequate description of the best scientific way of knowing. The MH method is better. The MH method is the best method for producing strong inferences about nature.

Summary

The first expressions of the hypothetico-deductive method have been traced as far back as to Christiaan Huygens in the seventeenth century (www.britannica.com/science/hypothetico-deductive-method). And the H-D method remains prominent as a description of the scientific method even today. With its frequent description on the web and in textbooks, the H-D method has become synonymous with the scientific method. "the hypothetico-deductive model seems genuinely to reflect scientific practice, which is perhaps why it has become the scientists' philosophy of science" (Lipton, 2004, p. 15). But in spite of its celebrity, the H-D method is not the best method for scientific inquiry. I will present the multiple hypothesis (MH) method as a preferred alternative to the H-D method. The H-D method focuses on a single hypothesis at a time, in isolation. To justify beliefs about reality and thereby produce strong inferences about the state of nature, the MH method considers not just a single hypothesis, but the collection of all plausible alternative hypotheses.

Chapter 3

The Method of Multiple Hypotheses

Prosecutors trying to convict a suspect of a crime need to be concerned not just with demonstrating that evidence points towards (rules in) the suspect or suspects as potential perpetrators of the crime. Prosecutors also need to be concerned with demonstrating that evidence excludes (rules out) everyone else as perpetrators. Otherwise, a defense attorney can raise doubt in the minds of the jurors about the guilt of the suspect or suspects by raising the possibility of alternative perpetrators. Unless the guilt of the suspect or suspects is shown to be substantially more likely than the guilt of other potential suspects, the prosecutor is not likely to win a conviction. Such are the reasons why fingerprints and DNA evidence are so powerful in court. Because DNA and fingerprints are unique to each person, they not only help rule in a suspect as a perpetrator, they also help rule out everyone else. And such are the reasons why criminal detectives go to such lengths to obtain DNA, fingerprints, and other uniquely winnowing evidence.

Similarly, doctors trying to identify the cause of an illness need to be concerned not just with finding that evidence points toward (rules in) a given disease as a potential cause of an illness. Doctors also need to try to demonstrate that the evidence excludes (rules out) other potential causes of the illness. Otherwise, a doctor risks treating the wrong cause of illness and leaving a patient's health unimproved or worse. Such are the reasons why diagnostic tests specific to different diseases are developed and why patients often undergo batteries of diagnostic tests.

In much the same way, scientists trying to explain a phenomenon need to be concerned not just with collecting data that support (rule in) a given hypothesis as an explanation for the phenomenon. Scientists also need to be concerned with collecting data that exclude (rule out) alternative hypotheses as explanations. For example, scientists so strongly believe the theory of evolution through natural selection not just because voluminous evidence is consistent with that theory but because they cannot identify alternative theories that fit the available data nearly as well (Dawkins, 2009). Scientists have diligently tried to identify alternatives to the theory of evolution through natural selection because the rewards for identifying a plausible alternative theory would be great. Alternative theories that have been entertained over time include the theory of creationism, intelligent design, Lamarkianism, and De Vries' mutation theory (Kean, 2012). And scientists have

DOI: 10.4324/9781003198413-3

been diligent in identifying and investigating implications of the theory of evolution through natural selection as well as implications of alternative theories. Finally, the evidence is in good agreement with the theory of evolution through natural selection and not in good agreement with any other identified alternatives. Hence, virtually all academic biologists believe, and are justified in believing, the theory of evolution through natural selection, until data suggest otherwise or a plausible alternative is identified. Should a truly viable alternative theory appear, scientists would not be justified in being as confident about the theory of evolution through natural selection. There is little rational warrant for believing one explanation for a phenomenon is true if two or more explanations are equally consistent with the available evidence.

The Method of Multiple Hypotheses Explained

The concern for ruling out alternatives (whether potential criminal suspects, illnesses, or scientific hypotheses) is shared not just by lawyers, doctors, and scientists but by anyone genuinely seeking to know what is true about reality, including philosophers, engineers, automobile mechanics, and most, if not all, others. The process of ruling in a hypothesis and ruling out alternative hypotheses to justify a belief that is shared by knowledge seekers can be explicated as follows.

To warrant the belief that hypothesis X explains a given phenomenon:

1. Diligently identify plausible alternatives to hypothesis X that could explain the given phenomenon.
2. Diligently obtain evidence relevant to hypothesis X and to the plausible alternatives to hypothesis X.
3. After completing Steps 1 and 2 above, a researcher is justified in tentatively accepting hypothesis X, if the evidence is in good agreement with hypothesis X and in not nearly as good agreement with any of the alternatives to hypothesis X.

This is the process of belief justification that I label the multiple hypotheses (MH) method.

Different fields of science have different hypotheses and different methods for collecting and interpreting empirical data. But it is my contention that all science ultimately justifies claims about phenomena using the method of multiple hypotheses. And this is not just true for science. As noted above, many fields besides science, including law and medicine at their best, ultimately reach conclusions about reality based on the method of multiple hypotheses.

In brief, two conditions must be met to justify believing that hypothesis X about a phenomenon in the natural world is true. First, evidence must be in good agreement with hypothesis X. Second, evidence must not be in as good agreement with alternatives to hypothesis X as with hypothesis X. Researchers are justified in believing a hypothesis if it is good at explaining diligently collected evidence and better at doing so than are diligently identified alternative hypotheses. To justify belief in a hypothesis, the hypothesis is placed in a survival-of-the-fittest competition with alternatives based on empirical evidence. In natural evolution, species survive or die because of their fit to their environments. In justifying beliefs, alternative hypotheses survive or die because of their fit to empirical data. Van Fraassen (1980) draws the same analogy between the scientific method and evolution by natural selection:

> I claim that the success of current scientific theories is no miracle. It is not even surprising to the scientific (Darwinist) mind. For any scientific theory is born into a life of fierce competition, a jungle red in tooth and claw. Only the successful theories survive—the ones which *in fact* latched on to actual regularities in nature.
>
> (p. 40, emphasis in original)

Popper (1968) offers the same perspective:

> According to my proposal, what characterizes the empirical method is its manner of exposing to falsification, in every conceivable way, the system to be tested. Its aim is not to save the lives of untenable systems but, on the contrary, to select the one which is by comparison the fittest, by exposing them all to the fiercest struggle for survival.
>
> (p. 42)

Note that *hypothesis* as used in the preceding definition of the method of multiple hypotheses could just as well be replaced with other terms such as theory, explanation, proposition, interpretation, and description. In other words, the process of belief justification is the process of justifying belief in all things such as hypotheses, theories, explanations, propositions, interpretations, and descriptions of the world. For ease of explication, I intend the word hypothesis to encompass all of the alternative terms. If you open your eyes and conclude that you see a computer, that qualifies as a hypothesis. So a hypothesis can be a simple description. Or it could be an elaborate theory such as quantum mechanics or the special and general theories of relativity. I mean for all such speculations about reality to fall under the rubric of a hypothesis, though I might sometimes use other terms. Warranting a belief, whether of a hypothesis, theory, explanation, proposition, interpretation, or description, involves putting alternatives into the survival-of-the-fittest competition described above.

Step 1 of the Multiple Hypotheses Method

The first step in the multiple hypotheses (MH) method is to diligently identify plausible alternatives to hypothesis X that could explain the phenomenon under question. The requirement that alternative hypotheses be plausible is an important one. The reason why plausibility is important is that it can be argued there are always literally innumerable hypotheses that could explain any given phenomenon. "Given any finite body of data, an infinite number of theories may be tailored to fit the body" (Garrison, 1986, p. 14). For example, dreams and hallucinations are always possible alternative hypotheses for any set of data. To produce an infinite number of alternative hypotheses, a researcher could propose the phenomena under question might be different combinations of dreams and hallucinations. For example, the experience of a phenomenon might be, it could be argued, 1% dream and 99% hallucination, or 2% dream and 98% hallucination, and so on. Another favorite alternative hypothesis of philosophers of science, which can be added to the list of possible options, is the brain-in-a-vat explanation which is the hypothesis that a person's brain has been removed, placed in a vat of sustaining fluid, and its perceptions and thoughts electrochemically controlled by a computer or some other external force. In the brain-in-the-vat explanation, no external reality is ever perceived so all explanations for phenomena, other than that the brain is in a vat, are false. Much the same holds true for Descartes' hypothesis of the workings of an evil demon and the machinations in the movies of the *Matrix* series.

Note that Step1 in the method of multiple hypotheses specifies that the alternative hypotheses that are to be identified are plausible. If the criterion that alternative hypotheses must be plausible were not included as part of Step 1 in the MH method, a problem for the multiple hypotheses method would immediately arise. The problem is that it would be impossible to implement the multiple hypotheses method with an infinite number of alternative hypotheses. Instead of considering an infinity of alternative hypotheses, a filter is applied when qualifying an alternative hypothesis to be entered into the subsequent survival-of-the-fittest competition (Campbell, 1988d). A hypothesis is deemed plausible only to the extent it agrees with currently available evidence and with well accepted theory, which are well accepted because they are, in turn, justified by available evidence. If a hypothesis comes to mind that is implausible, it is discarded right at the start. To summarize, only plausible hypotheses are considered in the MH method's survival-of-the-fittest competition which means the application of the multiple hypotheses method allows implausible hypotheses, should they come to mind, to be quickly dismissed based on available evidence and theory. Only plausible hypotheses are deemed to pass muster and placed in a survival-of-the-fittest competition. To reach the conclusion, in Step 3 of the MH method, that hypothesis X is accepted is to deem it the most plausible hypothesis of all initially plausible hypotheses, based on the available data and theorizing. As Lipton (2004) explained:

> We must use some sort of short list mechanism, where our background beliefs help us to generate a very limited list of plausible hypotheses, from which we then choose. … We consider only the few potential explanations of what we observe that seem reasonably plausible.
>
> (pp. 149–150)

Rosenberg (2012) even argues that considering only plausible hypotheses is part of our naturally evolved intellectual heritage: "We have been selected for entertaining only those alternative theories it is worth considering" (p. 247).

By emphasizing that only plausible hypotheses need to be put into the MH method's survival-of-the-fittest competition, it becomes evident there no longer is an infinite number of hypotheses available to be considered. Just the opposite might be the case. "Often, the scientist's problem is not to choose between many equally attractive theoretical systems, but to find even one" (Lipton, 2004, p. 174). Indeed, it might take a stroke of genius to come up with even a single plausible hypothesis that is consistent with available data and theorizing (Campbell, 1974, 1988d; Toulmin, 1961). For example, it took a genius to generate Newton's laws of motion to which there were no competitors for hundreds of years, until another genius proposed Einstein's theory of relativity.

When only a single plausible hypothesis is available, the researcher implements the multiple hypotheses method in abbreviated form. This means my description of the multiple hypotheses method is in need of a simplification, which should be obvious. If only a single plausible hypothesis is available, after a diligent search, a researcher is justified in tentatively accepting that hypothesis based on how well it conforms to diligently obtained evidence. I will say more about a single plausible hypothesis in a later chapter.

Of course, it is possible that a hypothesis judged implausible at one point in time, based on the data and the theorizing currently available, might later be deemed plausible based on additional data or theorizing. Such a redemption of a hypothesis can occur because the process of diligently identifying alternative hypotheses includes considering hypotheses that were once rejected. Indeed, a hypothesis judged implausible at one point in time might later be deemed the correct hypothesis, as affirmed by subsequent data and theorizing. This happened, for example, with the theory of continental drift. When the theory of continental drift was first proposed, it was considered implausible because there was no known mechanism that would allow continents to move. But later, the theory was resurrected when a mechanism for continental drift was identified, and the theory is now widely accepted. The point is that the method of multiple hypotheses allows for theories to be resurrected that, at an earlier point in time, had been initially judged implausible.

I should also note that alternative hypotheses are sometimes combined into a single hypothesis, which might be called the *opposite* hypothesis. For example, an investigation of the cause of an apparently mysterious phenomenon might be that extra-sensory perception exists. There will likely be any number of alternative explanations for such a phenomenon but all the alternatives might, for now, be lumped into the singular, opposite alternative that extra-sensory perception does not exist. In this way, the comparison that is being drawn is between just two hypotheses, where one of the two represents many alternatives. Or for convenience, I might direct attention to just two hypotheses for illustration, even though many more are possible. For example, I will shortly consider the choice between a flat and a round earth, even though there are many versions of both, including one that the earth is an oblate ellipsoid rather than a perfectly circular sphere.

That Step 1 of the method of multiple hypotheses requires diligence in identifying plausible alternative hypotheses is also critical. Diligence in identifying alternative hypotheses entails two processes. First, diligent identification means thorough discovery or creation of plausible hypotheses at the start of applying the method of multiple hypotheses. Second, diligent identification also means constantly seeking to identify and re-identify plausible hypotheses as the method proceeds. Diligent identification of alternative hypotheses means that Step 1 in the method of multiple hypotheses is to be repeated iteratively, especially when new data and theorizing become available. Indeed, all the steps in the method of multiple hypotheses are to be repeated iteratively, continually considering or reconsidering alternative hypotheses, including alternative hypotheses that either were initially deemed implausible or that had previously lost a survival-of-the-fittest competition. One place to look for *new* hypotheses is in the scrap-pile of formerly discarded hypotheses.

Diligence in searching for plausible alternative hypotheses means that researchers acquire as broad an array of plausible alternative hypotheses as possible. Having many hypotheses available is the best way to ensure a true hypothesis will be among the hypotheses that are being considered and ultimately selected. "The hypothesis that resists disproof in this Darwinian selection among 'multiple working hypotheses,' has a much better chance of being the right answer than if you had simply run with the first idea that caught your fancy" (Sagan, 1995, p. 210). Or as two time Nobel laureate Linus Pauling is often credited with proclaiming, "The way to get good ideas is to get lots of ideas, and throw the bad ones away."

Step 2 of the Multiple Hypotheses Method

The second step in the MH method is to diligently obtain empirical evidence relevant to hypothesis X, along with empirical evidence relevant to the alternatives to hypothesis X that were identified in Step 1. The purpose of diligently obtaining relevant empirical evidence is to ensure that all the plausible hypotheses have been effectively put through their paces before any one hypothesis is accepted. To ensure the accepted hypothesis has been properly vetted, diligence in obtaining relevant evidence means all the relevant evidence needed to choose among the plausible hypotheses has been collected. In many cases, the pool of relevant evidence is never exhausted and can never be completely exhausted. As a result, being diligent in collecting data means the search for data never ends. "As a hypothesis, the question of its truth or falsehood is open, and there is a continual search for more and more evidence to decide that question" (Copi, 1978, pp. 464–465). An implication of a never ending collection of data is that a hypothesis that is supported by currently available data might well be supplanted by a different hypothesis when additional data become available. So choosing among hypotheses is best accomplished by continuing to add more and more data.

The larger and more complex the relevant evidence, the easier it is to distinguish among hypotheses. Choosing a hypothesis to accept is a process of pattern matching (Campbell, 1966 1988e; Trochim, 1985). What a hypothesis implies about nature is matched with the obtained data. The more elaborate the pattern, the better the researcher can judge the plausibility of a hypothesis and distinguish among alternative hypotheses. That is, the more elaborate the pattern, the greater the confidence researchers can have that they have found the proper match. "The more complex the pattern that is successfully predicted, the less likely it is that alternative explanations could generate the same pattern" (Shadish, Cook, & Campbell, 2002, p. 105). Fingerprints and DNA are compelling to police detectives, prosecutors and juries because they are complex patterns.

Evidence that is relevant to a hypothesis is often said to be an implication or consequence of the hypothesis. Here is an example. Consider the task of distinguishing between the two hypotheses that the earth is either round or flat. There is a large amount of data that is relevant to these two hypotheses and that distinguishes between them. My two favorite sources of evidence are the following. If the earth were flat, the sun would rise at the same time for everyone on the flat surface. In contrast, if the earth were round, the sun would rise at different times for people located at different positions on the earth. The same holds for when the sun would set. That the sun would either rise or set either at different times or at the same time are implications of the two hypotheses about the shape of the earth. Another implication of the earth being flat is that everyone on the surface would see the same celestial constellations at the same time each night. In contrast, if the earth were round, different celestial constellations (or no constellations at all) would be visible for people located at different positions on the earth's surface at the same time. Thus, the two hypotheses imply patterns in the data that are at odds. That the data agree with these implications of the hypothesis that the earth is round, rather than that the earth is flat, is one of many reasons to believe the earth is round rather than flat. Other data turn out the same way. In total, the multitude of available data support the conclusion the earth is round rather than flat—hence the widespread and justified belief that the earth is round rather than flat. The point is the following. One way to identify data that are relevant to a hypothesis is to identify the implications or consequences of the hypothesis.

Note that writers sometimes talk of the predictions of hypotheses rather than the implications or consequences of hypotheses. The term prediction is sometimes taken to refer only to future events. But that is not always intended when talking of assessing hypotheses. Predictions can be the same as implications or consequences whether they are past, present, or future occurrences. I use the terms implications and consequences to avoid confusion about whether future predictions are intended. But predictions of hypotheses are sometimes easier to understand than implications or consequences of hypotheses. So if talking about implications and consequences seems at all opaque, think in terms of predictions whether they be past, present, or future.

Although thinking of implications or consequences is a useful way to go about identifying data relevant to a hypothesis, it can also be useful to identify data relevant to a hypothesis by thinking in the reverse order. That is, in addition to deducing empirical implications from a hypothesis think in the reverse fashion—deducing hypotheses from empirical data. The reason to think in the reverse order is that sometimes you might best recognize data that are relevant to a hypothesis not by thinking of implications of the hypothesis but by recognizing, in reverse order, that the data imply the hypothesis (Lipton, 2004, Walton, 2005). For example, consider distinguishing between the two hypotheses—that extrasensory perception (ESP) exists and that ESP does not exist. ESP includes the purported ability to know the future which is called precognition. To identify data that can be used to distinguish between these hypotheses, one approach is to think of implications or consequences of the two hypotheses. An alternative approach would be to recognize data and see what they imply about the two hypotheses. In different circumstances, one approach might be more fruitful than the other. For example, if you were to think of implications of ESP it might not occur to you that casinos would go out of business if people could know future outcomes of a roulette wheel before they take place. But if, while gambling, you were to contemplate that casinos are profitable, you might recognize that such an outcome suggests that precognition does not exist. The point is the following. To identify data relevant to hypotheses, think of data that are implied by the hypotheses as well as hypotheses that are implied by data.

Perhaps another example will help make the preceding distinction clear. In the mid-1800s, Ignaz Semmelweis hypothesized that having physicians wash their hands before assisting in child birth would reduce the incidence of puerperal fever. The reason, of course, is that dirty hands transmit germs. As a result, data that support the germ theory of disease also support Semmelweis' hypothesis or, in the nomenclature of the MH method, data that support the germ theory are relevant to Semmelweis' theory. But the germ theory of disease is not so much a consequence of Semmelweis' hypothesis as the other way around. Semmelweis' hypothesis follows from the germ theory of disease. Data strongly supported Semmelweis' hypothesis during his lifetime. But his hypothesis was not widely accepted until the germ theory was propounded after his death. Once data in support of the germ theory became available, Semmelweis' previous hypothesis was widely accepted. It was easy to see how Semmelweis' hypothesis follows from the germ theory. It was not as easy to see, at least not at the time, how the germ theory follows from Semmelweis' hypothesis. The point is the following. Data supporting the germ theory are relevant to Semmelweis' hypothesis even though the germ theory is not obviously an implication or consequence of Semmelweis' hypothesis.

Or consider the example of the kinetic versus the caloric theory of heat. The kinetic theory specifies that heat is a result of the movement of molecules while the caloric theory specifies that heat is a result of a substance called caloric which passes from hotter to colder bodies (Goldstein & Goldstein, 1984). The findings of quantum mechanics, which describe the behavior of molecules, are relevant to discriminating between the two theories. But the findings of quantum mechanics are not so much an implication or consequence of the kinetic theory as the opposite: the kinetic theory of heat is a consequence or implication of the theory of quantum mechanics.

To summarize: one way to identify data relevant to a hypothesis is to think through implications or consequences of the hypothesis. But implications and consequences of a hypothesis are not necessarily the only data relevant to a hypothesis. Any data that either lends support to or casts doubt upon a hypothesis is relevant to that hypothesis. When I talk, in Step 2 of the MH method, of diligently obtaining evidence relevant to hypothesis X and to the alternatives to hypothesis X, I include identifying implications and consequences of the hypotheses. But also think in the opposite fashion. To identify data relevant to hypotheses think of data implied by hypotheses as well as hypotheses implied by data.

It is worth nothing that the hypothetico-deductive method, both as described and as even implied by its name, specifies that evidence relevant to a hypothesis is to be deduced from the hypothesis under study. But, as just noted, it need not be the case that relevant evidence is deduced from the hypotheses under study. The MH method is described explicitly in terms of relevant evidence rather than deduced evidence. Hence, the MH method allows for evidence to be obtained either by deduction from hypothesis to evidence or by the reverse process. In contrast, the hypothetico-deductive method is described as if, and as its name suggests, relevant evidence is only to be deduced from the hypothesis under investigation.

Step 3 of the Multiple Hypotheses Method

In step 3, the obtained evidence is examined to see whether it well supports one hypothesis and doesn't well support any others. "The trick is to hold on to several possible (rival) explanations until one of them gets increasingly more compelling as the result of more, stronger, and varied sources of evidence" (Miles & Huberman, 1994, p. 275). Only if the evidence supports one hypothesis better than it supports the other available hypotheses is a researcher justified in choosing that one hypothesis over the others.

In the hypothetico-deductive (H-D) method, when data agree with the hypothesis under investigation, the conclusion to be reached might be phrased differently by different writers. According to different proposals, a hypothesis under investigation that is found to be in agreement with the data might alternatively be said to be accepted, confirmed, not rejected, supported, corroborated, retained, or justified, and the like. Conversely, a hypothesis that is found not to be in agreement with its investigated implications could alternatively be said to be refuted, disconfirmed, rejected, or contradicted, and the like.

Some writers, it seems, would be happy to use such terms interchangeably. Other writers are not as happy. Popper (1968), for example, initially used *confirmed* but later decided that *corroborated* had importantly different connotations and was the preferred choice when a hypothesis was in agreement with the evidence. In contrast, I do not distinguish among the various terms in the context of Step 3 of the multiple hypotheses method. I am happy to use any of the terms. Most often, I will talk of accepting hypothesis X when the method of multiple hypotheses has been applied and the criteria for ruling in hypothesis X and ruling out alternative hypotheses have been satisfied in Step 3. In any case, it is important to understand what it means to accept hypothesis X.

When I speak of hypothesis X being accepted in Step 3, I do not mean that we have to accept hypothesis X as literally true. It would be nice if hypothesis X were true. And hypothesis X might well be true. But to accept hypothesis X means merely that researchers will use that hypothesis in making decisions and taking actions at the present time. People often need to make decisions and take actions. In doing so, people should use the best knowledge they have about the world. It is in the sense of using the best knowledge available that I say a person is justified in accepting a hypothesis using the method of multiple hypotheses. If people are building a bridge, they need to utilize the best knowledge available about how to build safe and reliable bridges. In accepting hypothesis X, I propose people use hypothesis X as if it were true without having necessarily to believe it is literally true.

Please be careful about what I am and am not saying about believing a hypothesis is true. I am a realist and I believe in truth. I believe reality exists and that hypotheses can be true in that they can correspond exactly to reality. As I sit in my office writing this, I believe I am typing on a computer and I believe my assessment is 100% correct. But I might not always be correct in my beliefs. It is for this reason that accepting a hypothesis need not entail believing it is true. The history of science has too often taught researchers that even hypotheses well supported by evidence and currently without any plausible alternative hypotheses that are well supported by evidence can be wrong. And well supported hypotheses need not even be approximately true. By accepting a theory, I mean to accept it as if it were true without necessarily being committed to the belief that it is true. If a hypothesis passes the test of the method of multiple hypotheses, people are justified in making decisions and taking actions, when they need to do so at the present time, as if the hypothesis were true even though people need not be confident the hypothesis is perfectly true.

Accepting a Hypothesis without the Diligent Application of the Method of Multiple Hypotheses

The method of multiple hypotheses is stringent in its requirements. The method of multiple hypotheses explicitly requires being diligent in identifying plausible alternative hypotheses and being diligent in obtaining data relevant to all the plausible hypotheses. Being truly diligent in either task can make the tasks never ending, which obviously makes the tasks impossible to complete in practice. In practice, researchers might not have even been capable of effectively exploring all the low hanging fruit of plausible hypotheses and relevant data. At different stages of investigation, limited sets of hypotheses and limited amounts of data might have been assessed and obtained. Researchers must be satisfied with doing what is possible in the time and resources available.

The implication is that researchers, and other interested parties such as policy makers, will need to make decisions or act when researchers have not been completely diligent in their identification and assessment of hypotheses. The time for making decisions is limited. Interested parties do not have the luxury of waiting until researchers have been completely diligent in their investigations. Nonetheless, interested parties can still be justified in accepting a hypothesis even though researchers have not been completely diligent in identifying and assessing hypotheses.

When interested parties have to make decisions and act, they should use the best information available and they are justified in doing so. To the extent whatever evidence is available agrees with hypothesis X better than with whatever alternative hypotheses have been identified, a person can be justified in tentatively accepting hypothesis X. But diligently completing the steps in the method of multiple hypotheses is the gold standard for justifying belief in a hypothesis—the ideal toward which to strive. The more diligently a researcher conducts the steps in the method of multiple hypotheses, the greater a researcher should be confident in accepting hypothesis X and in making decisions and taking action based on hypothesis X, even though belief in hypothesis X should always be tentative. Degree of belief should be apportioned according to the diligence with which the steps in the multiple hypotheses method have been performed. That the steps in the method of multiple hypotheses are not always carried out diligently does not invalidate the method. The method is prescriptive but not always descriptive.

It is also important to note that a researcher can be justified in accepting a hypothesis even when some of the available data do not well support the hypothesis. There are innumerable examples of subsequently well corroborated hypotheses that appeared at odds with some available data at one time or another (Chalmers, 2013). Indeed, Feyerabend (1975) insists "there is not a single interesting theory that agrees with all the known facts in its domain" (p. 31). An historical example is provided by the Darwinian theory of evolution. The theory of evolution through natural selection was at odds with what was believed, at one time, to be reliable evidence about the age of the earth. Yet Darwin continued to advocate his theory and it was subsequently determined that the earth was much older than had originally been thought. (The age of the earth was assumed to be limited by the age of the sun and the sun was thought to be much younger than it was before the discovery of nuclear energy.) So a researcher can be justified in accepting a hypothesis even in the face of some conflicting data though it is easiest to do so when the available data mostly support the hypothesis and less well support alternative hypotheses.

It might not be the case that diligently collected evidence perfectly favors one hypothesis over all others. Nonetheless, evidence should be used to decide which hypotheses to favor over others. It is rational to favor those hypotheses that are most plausible in light of the available evidence. But when they do not have compelling evidence, people should be especially cautious in their beliefs.

The Single Cause Fallacy

It is important to understand what can qualify as a hypothesis so as not to commit the single cause fallacy (Stanovich, 2004). A hypothesis under investigation might specify the cause or causes of a phenomenon. Ruling out alternative hypotheses in favor of a hypothesis X does not mean that a phenomenon can have only a single cause. Rather, it is possible for hypothesis X to specify that multiple causes are operating. Let me be a little more specific. Suppose a researcher is entertaining the possibility that a phenomenon might be caused by A and/or B. A variety of hypotheses might be entertained. One hypothesis is that neither A nor B is the cause. A second hypothesis is that A but not B is the cause. A third hypothesis is that B but not A is the cause. A fourth hypothesis is that A and B are both causes. Any of these hypotheses could serve as hypothesis X in the multiple hypotheses method. And the remainder of the hypotheses, among others, would be alternatives to hypothesis X. In particular, hypothesis X might be that both A and B are causes so the conclusion to be reached is that multiple causes are operating. The point is that accepting a hypothesis about causality, and ruling out alternative hypotheses, need not mean that a phenomenon can have only a single cause. An eligible, and potentially true, hypothesis could be that more than a single cause is operating, in which case the hypotheses that only single causes are operating would be alternative hypotheses.

Other Criteria for Belief Justification

According to the method of multiple hypotheses, as I have presented it, the only criteria for justifying belief in a hypothesis are good agreement between the accepted hypothesis and available data and correspondingly poor agreement between alternative hypotheses and the available data. Numerous other criteria have been proposed for justifying belief in hypotheses besides agreement with data. Other proposed criteria include that the favored hypothesis be simple, elegant, precise, generative (i.e., leading to additional implications and theories), consistent with other theories, and wide ranging in its affirmed implications (Frank, 1956; Hempel, 1966; Kuhn, 1998[1977]; Newton-Smith, 1981). All these criteria make sense. But the bottom line is, and must be, agreement with empirical evidence. Science

> is based on the principle that observation is the judge of whether something is so or not .... observation is the ultimate and final judge of the truth of an idea.
>
> (Feynman, 1998, p. 15)

Consider, for example, simplicity as a criterion for the acceptability of a hypothesis. Occam's razor is well recognized as giving priority to simplicity over complexity. But a hypothesis well supported by data that is relatively complex should still be accepted ahead of a relatively simple theory that is not as well supported by data. That is, simplicity should not be favored over accuracy—a hypothesis should be simple but not too simple to plausibly explain the data. Or as Einstein is said to have proclaimed, "Everything should be as simple as it can be, but not simpler." If a hypothesis is too simple to fit the data, agreement with the data ultimately should win out over simplicity.

Or consider the criterion of agreement with other well validated theories. For a theory to be well validated means the theory is in good agreement with evidence. For a hypothesis to be in agreement with other theories means the hypothesis is in agreement with the data that support the other theories, which is what the MH method espouses. The final arbiter of the acceptability of hypotheses is empirical data, as specified by the MH method (Pierce, 1897/1931; Potochnick et al., 2019).

Perhaps I should note that in practice non-epistemic forces often play a role in choosing among hypotheses. For example, what is called the strong program in the sociology of scientific knowledge specifies that theory choice is often determined by such things as faith, prejudice, politics, material reward, social status, and the desire for fame and power (Klee, 1997; Rosenberg, 2012). (The strong program also emphasizes that hypotheses are constructed by investigators rather than discovered in nature.) Certainly non-empirical factors do influence theory choice. But a prescriptive, rather than descriptive, theory choice would emphasize the preeminence of the multiple hypotheses method with its insistence on the preeminence of data in reaching conclusions. "In the long run, then, the ultimate test of the superiority of one theory over another is observational success" (Newton-Smith, 1981, p. 224).

The Tentative Acceptance of a Hypothesis

As I have specified in the method of multiple hypotheses, the conclusion to accept a hypothesis is always made tentatively. A conclusion is made tentatively (or provisionally) because the process of belief justification is never complete. A researcher can never know if all plausible alternative hypotheses have been identified. Perhaps the correct hypothesis for a phenomenon has yet to be discovered/invented and investigated. And researchers can always obtain more data relevant to a hypothesis. Perhaps a favored hypothesis is well supported by all the available data but would be contraindicated by new data, were they available. At one point, the available data might suggest that hypothesis X should be accepted. While at another time, additional data might suggest that hypothesis X is incorrect and that alternative hypothesis Y should be accepted instead. And still later, hypothesis X might be rejuvenated based on further data. To use an analogy from criminal investigations, the evidence might at first point convincingly at Ms. X as the murderer. But additional evidence might suggest Ms. X is being framed by Mr. Y, only later to find a further double cross is involved.

As will be explained in a later chapter, neither the method of multiple hypotheses nor any other method can prove that a hypothesis is correct. As a result, any conclusion that is reached could be incorrect. Without all possible hypotheses and all possible data being available, researchers should never unconditionally accept a hypothesis as true. So any conclusion must be made tentatively.

The history of science well illustrates the twists and turns that can take place in reaching conclusions and reveals the fallacy of either accepting or rejecting hypotheses irrevocably. Newtonian mechanics was accepted as undeniably true for a couple centuries before it was overturned by relativity theory. Conversely, the theory of continental drift was denied for decades because it appeared at odds with the available evidence. Not only was no evidence for any mechanisms of continental drift available but mechanisms for continental drift were considered inconceivable when the theory was first introduced. Yet subsequent data have substantially corroborated the theory. It is appropriate to persistently challenge a revered hypothesis and it is appropriate to reconsider a previously discredited hypothesis. A hypothesis that seemed either plausible or implausible at one point in time, may look either less or more plausible in the face of new data.

The search for alternative hypotheses and the search for data with which to assess those hypotheses is to continue diligently without end. This is, of course, impossible. We cannot wait until eternity before making decisions and taking action in the present. But because the process of belief justification never ends, ultimate decisions about which hypotheses to accept must always be tentative—no final decisions about which hypotheses to accept can ever be made. New data or new hypotheses might emerge later. Conclusion must always be open to revision. It is always possible that a new hypothesis will come along that better explains our observations and which shows that our most cherished and trusted beliefs are wrong. Popper (1968) likens science to a game that continues indefinitely: "He who decides one day that scientific statements do not call for any further test, and that they can be regarded as finally verified, retires from the game" (p. 53).

Breaking the Rules (in the Short Term)

Some have argued the scientific method has no rules or restrictions. For example, Bridgman (1955) has famously announced: "The scientific method, as far as it is a method, is nothing more than doing one's damnedest with one's mind, no holds barred." Similarly, Feyerabend (1975) is famous for arguing that good scientific practice does not follow any universal rules. As a result, it is said that researchers should feel free to break any and all methodological rules that have been propounded for conducting science. For example, a strict falsificationist approach to science specifies that hypotheses are refuted once disconfirming data are discovered. But, as we have seen, this rule often has and often should be broken. That is, hypotheses that have, at one point, apparently failed empirical tests have sometimes later been shown to be in better agreement with the data than are alternatives to that hypothesis. Accordingly, researchers might wish to violate the tenants of the method of multiple hypotheses, for example, by favoring hypothesis A over hypothesis B even though the data available at the moment offer better support for hypothesis B. So be it. But such rule breaking may occur only in the short term.

In the short run, it can be useful and appropriate to break rules. But that doesn't mean rules are useless or inappropriate. In football, it can be a wise strategy to break the rules on pass interference when it would save a touchdown. But the general prohibition against breaking the rules applies in most situations in football. Teams that receive more penalties for breaking the rules tend to lose more often than teams that do not break the rules as often and receive as many penalties. Just because rules are often broken to good effect does not mean there are no sets of rules that work well. The multiple hypotheses method offers one such set of rules that work well. Feyerabend (1975) argues for anarchy in scientific methods and counterintuitive approaches for knowledge generation because such lawless strategies sometimes work. But that such strategies work at times does not mean they should be used as general practice. Staley (2014) argued that even though a rule might be fallible at times does not mean it is flawed as a general principle: "In particular, if following a methodological rule yields *reliable* results, or results more reliable than those observed by alternative methods, then it is reasonable for scientists to follow that rule" (p. 89, emphasis in original). In the long term, the method of multiple hypotheses provides the best rules of the game and provides the most reliable results. In the end, the MH method is and should be the final arbiter of which hypotheses to accept and which to reject.

Inference to the Best Explanation

The multiple hypotheses method might be likened to the method of inference called inference to the best explanation, which is also sometimes called abductive inference (Josephson, 1994; but see Mcauliffe, 2015). Harman (1965) is often credited as the originator of the method of inference to the best explanation. He explains that a researcher must consider and reject alternative explanations before "one infers, from the premise that a given hypothesis would provide a 'better' explanation for the evidence than would any other hypothesis, to the conclusion that the given hypothesis is true" (Harmon, 1965, p. 89). And Lipton (2004, p. 1) provides examples of inference to the best explanation:

> Faced with tracks in the snow of a certain peculiar shape, I infer that a person on snowshoes has recently passed this way. There are other possibilities, but I make this inference because it provides the best explanation of what I see. Watching me pull my hand away from the stove, you infer that I am in pain, because this is the best explanation of my excited behavior.
>
> (p. 1)

But as typically described, inference to the best explanation is not the same as the MH method. A primary difference between the two methods of inference is that, unlike my depiction of the MH method, descriptions of inference to the best explanation do not usually emphasize diligently obtaining data with which to choose among alternative hypotheses. As depicted, inference to the best explanation seems to focus on available evidence without directing researchers to collect additional evidence. With inference to the best explanation there is also less emphasis on an elaborated and sustained survival-of-the-fittest competition. Perhaps inference to the best explanation can be considered a component of the MH method. And explications of inference to the best explanation can enlighten understanding of the MH method. But, as presented, inference to the best explanation is not the entirety of the MH method.

Disputatious Communities of Scholars

The MH method need not be implemented by a lone investigator. Indeed, being diligent in identifying and investigating alternative hypotheses is often best accomplished by groups of investigators. Campbell (1984) talked of requiring a disputatious community of scholars to best justify one's own hypotheses and challenge the favored hypotheses of others. It might well be impossible to avoid Chamberlin's (1890/1965) fears that investigators will be emotionally biased toward some hypotheses more than others, in spite of one's best efforts to remain neutral and keep multiple hypotheses in mind. As a result, the surest path to strong inference is likely via a community of scholars committed to critiquing and expanding upon the work of their colleagues by proposing and investigating alternative hypotheses. Even if scholars investigated only their own favored hypotheses, the conglomerate of investigations could still accomplish the multiple hypotheses method. Each investigator might engage in the H-D method. But as a whole, science would progress using the MH method. So the scientific way of knowing is still best described as the method of multiple hypotheses.

Attempts to Justify the Hypothetico-Deductive Method

Sometimes multiple hypotheses are easy to come by, but not always. In some cases, as I have already noted, it might require a stroke of genius to come up with even a single plausible hypothesis to account for a given phenomenon much less to come up with a multitude of plausible alternatives hypotheses. When only a single plausible hypothesis is available that hypothesis is assessed without being placed in an explicit competition among alternative hypotheses. A critic of my argument might suggest that, in such cases, the MH method is indistinguishable from the H-D method. I must demur for two reasons. First, even when only a single plausible hypothesis is available the MH method differs from the H-D method. For example, the MH method insists that researchers diligently assess all relevant data while the H-D method, as typically presented, does not. Second, the MH method insists the researcher continually try to identify alternative hypotheses while the H-D method, as typically presented, does not. Even if no plausible alternative hypotheses are available at the moment, it may be possible to come up with some in the future. As a result, even when only a single plausible hypotheses is available at the moment, researchers should still conceptualize the task of empirical research as following the MH method rather than the H-D method.

Alternatively, an advocate of the H-D method might argue that the H-D method is a component of the larger MH method so the MH method consists of nothing more than performing the H-D method repeatedly. To some extent, such a critic is correct. It is indeed the case that, at various points in time, a researcher who uses the MH method might well be concerned with a single hypothesis, a single implication of that hypothesis, and a single set of data with which to assess that hypothesis, without focusing on alternative hypotheses, multiple implications, or a broad collection of data. In those instances, the MH method might be little more than the H-D method. For example, a study might be focused on either ruling in or ruling out a specific hypothesis without being concerned, at the moment, with any other alternative hypotheses. This is akin to a police detective checking an alibi to see if a person can be either ruled in or ruled out as a potential suspect without concern, at the moment, with whether any other potential suspects have adequate alibis. This is also akin to a doctor running laboratory tests whose purpose is either to rule in or to rule out a disease without being concerned, at the moment, with the possibility of other diseases or other tests. In such cases, the actions of the scientist, police detective, and doctor can be conceptualized as an implementation of little more than the H-D method.

But sooner or later, scientists, police detectives, and doctors need to consider additional implications of the hypothesis under investigation at the moment and whether alternative hypotheses are just as plausible. As it is presented in the literature, the H-D method does neither. The H-D method, as usually described in the literature, considers a single hypothesis in isolation and considers a limited set of implications of that hypothesis and a restricted set of data to assess those implications. Considering a single hypothesis in isolation is not the same as being consciously aware of the need to assess alternative hypotheses as in the MH method. For example, being aware of alternative hypotheses encourages researchers to focus on assessing implications that serve to discriminate among hypotheses. As a result, the MH method is greater than the sum of H-D components. If the H-D method were meant to be applied repeatedly wherein the researcher focused on competing alternative hypotheses, diligently contemplating relevant implications of those hypotheses (especially those implications that discriminate among alternative hypotheses), and pursuing the reams of data needed to accomplish such tasks, the H-D method should be described that way. Because it is not described that way, the H-D method is not the MH method.

Or an advocate of the H-D method might argue it is implicit in the H-D method that researchers would consider alternative hypotheses, derive multiple implications, and collect accompanying data, as in the MH method. If so, it would be better to make explicit the need to investigate alternative hypotheses as in the MH method rather than to leave that need implicit as in the H-D method. Any attempt to depict the process of belief justification should place alternative hypotheses front and center. It is the MH method rather than the H-D method that does so.

Summary

Two conditions must be met to justify believing that hypothesis X about the natural world is true. First, the available evidence must be in good agreement with hypothesis X. Second, the available evidence must not be in as good agreement with alternatives to hypothesis X as with hypothesis X. The second condition specifies that justifying a belief in hypothesis X requires putting plausible alternative hypotheses to hypothesis X into an empirical survival-of-the-fittest competition with hypothesis X to ensure hypothesis X agrees with the evidence better than does any alternative hypothesis. When diligent in satisfying the two conditions, researchers are justified in tentatively accepting the proposed hypothesis as true. In simple terms: "You think of as many hypotheses as you can, then you design experiments to test them to see which are true and which are false" (Pirsig, 1999, p. 109). The strategy just described is called the method of multiple hypotheses.

Chapter 4

Examples of the Multiple Hypotheses Method

As noted in Chapter 2, the hypothetico-deductive method is often described as the scientific method and such descriptions of the H-D method are particularly common in websites and textbooks. Nonetheless, as emphasized in Chapter 1 and in many quotations elsewhere in the text, I am not the only person to emphasize the need to consider multiple hypotheses (as in the MH method), rather than a single hypothesis (as in the H-D method), when justifying beliefs about nature. In addition, it is common practice in research to use the multiple hypotheses method, rather than the H-D method. That is, alternative hypotheses are often taken into account in the best research practices, which is in keeping with the MH method, even if the scientific method is often not described as doing such. I could give many examples of research that embody the method of multiple hypotheses. The present chapter provides three illustrations.

Abortion and Crime

In a ground-breaking, best-selling book, Levitt and Dubner (2005) provide creative and surprising explanations for dozens of perplexing findings over the years. One puzzle concerned the causes of the dramatic reduction in crime in the U.S. during the 1990s.

As described in Levitt and Dubner (2005; Donohue & Levitt, 2001, 2020; Levitt, 2004), there had been a precipitous increase in crime in the U.S. leading up to the 1990s. Commentators were predicting catastrophic outcomes for the 1990s because of the preceding increases in crime. But the crime rate unexpectedly and dramatically turned down in the 1990s instead of continuing its frightening upward trend. Reasons for the drop in crime were forwarded. Levitt and Dubner had their own explanation. But to support their explanation, they first examined other potential hypotheses. Consider nine of the explanations, eight from others and the ninth from Levitt and Dubner. The point is that Levitt and Dubner implemented the multiple hypotheses method (though not without controversy in its interpretation, as discussed later) by showing that data well support their ninth explanation for why crime dropped precipitously in the 1990s, while showing that the other eight alternative explanations either do not

DOI: 10.4324/9781003198413-4

well account for any of the reduction in crime or leave a large proportion of the reduction in crime unexplained. I briefly review all nine hypotheses and some of the data used to interrogate them. The data Levitt and Dubner provide to support their conclusions are far more extensive than I report here.

Improved Economy. The U.S. economy was robust in the 1990s and there were plentiful jobs. It is reasonable to assume that the availability of jobs would mean there was less incentive to commit crimes for which there were monetary gains, and hence lead to a reduction in crime. That is, it could make sense for crimes like burglary to drop because there were better, less risky ways, to make money. But all crimes dropped in the 1990s and not just crimes for which there were monetary benefits. Given all the data, the effect of the growth in the economy was judged to be too weak to account for the massive drop in crime that occurred in the 1990s.

More Capital Punishment. The use of capital punishment had increased dramatically by the 1990s. One of the justifications for capital punishment is deterrence: Increasing the frequency of capital punishment should deter future capital crimes. But the number of executions during the 1990s was too small to produce a deterrence effect likely to significantly affect the overall crime rate. "It is extremely unlikely, therefore, that the death penalty, as currently practiced in the United States, exerts any real influence on crime rates" (Levitt & Dubner, 2005, p. 125).

Stricter Gun Control Policies. Stricter gun control policies could conceivably keep more guns out of the hands of criminals, hence reducing crime. And there were increased gun control policies enacted in the1990s. For example, the national Brady Act was meant to reduce the potential for criminals to buy guns by implementing background checks and outright bans on handguns were implemented in some locales. But the drop in crime in the 1990s preceded the Brady Act and the locales with bans tended to trail behind other locales in reducing crime. All told, the data do not well support the conclusion that changes in gun control policies were substantially responsible for the reduction in crime in the 1990s.

Aging Population. The theory of an aging population causing a reduction in crime is that the elderly are less likely than the young to commit crimes. In accordance with this theory, the U.S. population was, on average, aging in the 1990s. The problem with the aging-population theory, however, is that an abrupt drop in crime cannot well be explained by what was a gradual rise in the age of the population.

Innovations in Policing Strategies. Innovative policing strategies were implemented in the 1990s in some locales, such as New York City (NYC) where police cracked down on minor crimes on the theory that undeterred small crimes tend to lead to bigger ones. In what appears to support NYC's crackdown on crimes, crimes dropped dramatically in that city. But the innovations in policing in NYC mostly started in 1994 well after crime started to drop in the early 1990s. In addition, many other cities had dramatic reductions in crime without implementing changes in policing strategies. As a result, the data do not well support the conclusion that innovative policing activities contributed significantly to the reduction in crime in the 1990s.

More Police. Careful research demonstrates that putting more police on the streets reduces crime. In keeping with this inverse relationship, more police were on the streets in the 1990s and crime decreased as a result. Comparing crime rates in cities where police were added to crime rates in cities where police were not added, Levitt and Dubner (2005) conclude that about 10 percent of the reduction in crime in the 1990s was due to increases in the numbers of police.

Declining Drug Markets. Trafficking in crack cocaine was known to result in increased crime, especially homicides among drug dealers. In the 1990s, decreasing profits in selling cocaine contributed to a dramatic reduction in drug related homicides. Levitt and Dubner (2005) estimate that about 15 percent of the reduction in crime in the 1990s was due to the reduction in profits from selling of cocaine.

Increased Prison Population. One reason for the increase in crime during the 1960s was likely a reduction in the prison population due to changes in convictions and sentencing. These changes were reversed in the 1990s. For example, imprisonments for violating drug laws increased dramatically. Data suggest that stricter prison sentences lead to a reduction in crime due to either deterring crime or removing the opportunity for those in prison to commit crimes. Levitt and Dubner estimated that about a third of the reduction in crime in the 1990s was due to stricter prison sentencing.

Roe v. Wade. The 1973 Supreme Court decision of *Roe v. Wade* legalized abortion across the nation and, according to Levitt and Dubner (2005), was likely the major cause of the reduction in crime in the 1990s. The theory behind the argument that the legalization of abortion reduced crime is the following. Before *Roe v. Wade* many young, poor, single, and poorly educated women who were unable to obtain abortions gave birth to unwanted and relatively poorly cared for babies—and young, poor, single, and poorly educated mothers tend to have unwanted and poorly cared for children who subsequently turn into young adults who engage in significant crime. After *Roe v. Wade* the number of such unwanted births was greatly reduced because abortions became more widely available and less expensive for impoverished women. Because of the reduction in unwanted and poorly cared for babies who would have begun to commit crimes in earnest starting at about age seventeen, crime starting dropping in the early 1990s, seventeen years after the 1973 decision of *Roe v. Wade*.

In addition, extensive data suggest that the legalization of abortion accounted for the largest portion of the reduction of crime in the 1990s. Consider the following six findings.

1 Five states (Alaska, California, Hawaii, New York, and Washington) legalized abortion before *Roe v. Wade*. The reduction in crime in these states preceded the reduction in crime in other states.

2 Across states, the rate of abortion in the 1970s correlated negatively with the crime rate in the 1990s, but did not correlate with the crime rate before the 1990s.
3 Reductions in crime rates were greatest among younger, compared to older, people.
4 Similar relationships between rates of crime and abortion have been documented in Australia, Canada, Europe, and Scandinavia.
5 A draconian anti-abortion mandate was implemented in Romania in 1966 and Romanians were less likely to commit crimes if they were born before 1966 than after.
6 Data supporting the effects of abortion on crime have been extended into the last two decades (Donohue & Levitt, 2020).

Conclusions. Levitt and Dubner (2005) used the MH method in their argument that the reduction in the crime rates in the U.S. in the 1990s was substantially due to legalized abortion in 1973. Levitt and Dubner considered multiple hypotheses and used extensive data either to rule out alternative hypotheses or to show that alternative hypotheses were inadequate to explain much of the reduction in the crime rates in the 1990s. In turn, Levitt and Dubner used extensive data to rule in abortion as a plausible cause of a major portion of the reduction in crime.

I should note that Levitt and Dubner's (2005) conclusion about the effect of abortion on the U.S. crime rate has been criticized by numerous researchers and remains controversial (Foote & Goetz, 2008; Lott & Whitley, 2007). Analyses have been performed both with the same data that Levitt and Dubner used and with new data, including from Canada and England. Findings are contradictory. Some of the further research supports the Levitt and Dubner conclusions and some contests it. The point is that the causes of the decline in crime rate in the U.S. starting in the early 1990s remains under considerable debate. The purpose of my presentation is not to argue that the legalization of abortion contributed to the decline as Levitt and Dubner (2005) argue. My purpose is simply to illustrate the use of the MH method by Levitt and Dubner. Levitt and Dubner made their case by use of the MH method. If Levitt and Dubner are ultimately shown to be wrong, it will likely be by further use of the MH method.

Home Field Advantage in Sports

In a highly readable and engaging best-seller, Moskowitz and Wertheim (2011) tackle more than a dozen mystifying findings and myths in the international world of sports. The book both documents surprising outcomes and solves them by providing compelling explanations. One of the topics they address is the presence and cause of home field advantage in sports.

Home field (or home team) advantage means that the team at home wins sporting competitions more often than the team that is visiting. As Moskowitz and Wertheim (2011) document, a reliable home field advantage exists across a wide range of sports. Out of the nineteen international sports leagues that Moskowitz and Wertheim examine, the winning percentages for teams playing at home range from a low of 53 percent in the Japanese professional baseball league to a high of 69 percent in both college basketball and Major League Soccer, with professional hockey, football, rugby, and cricket lying in between those extremes. The question is: What is the cause of home field advantage?

To answer this question, Moskowitz and Wertheim (2011) followed the MH method. They diligently identified plausible alternative hypotheses to explain the phenomenon and diligently obtained relevant data with which to put the hypotheses into competition as explanations. Here are descriptions of the different hypotheses for home field advantage that Moskowitz and Wertheim (2011) identified with brief summaries of how well they survive in the face of relevant evidence.

Fans. Do cheers for the home team and boos for the visiting team contribute to home field advantage because they directly influence player performance? To avoid other potential influences, Moskowitz and Wertheim (2011) looked for performances by players that were independent of anything else going on during a game except for the effects of fan support on the players. In basketball, free throws are unencumbered by many other outside influences besides fan engagement. The same holds for shootouts at the ends of games in hockey, penalty kicks at the ends of games in soccer, and the speed and accuracy of pitches in baseball. If fan support was having an effect, home field advantage should be evident in such performances in the various sports. But home field advantage is not evident there. Fans may be cheering loudly but players at home appear to perform no better than players away from home as a result.

Travel. Travel can be tiring and disconcerting, and away teams have to travel to play games while members of home teams do not endure the travails of travel. But home field advantage is just as large when the visiting team comes from the same city as the home team, in which case travel is virtually the same for the two teams. Nor does home field advantage vary with the distances the away teams have to travel. Nor does home field advantage vanish in the National Football League (NFL) where away teams can travel a day or more before their weekly games and thereby be well rested after traveling. Home field advantage does not seem to be much due to the exertion of travel.

Home Field Characteristics. Baseball fields can differ widely from stadium to stadium and teams might build their teams with hitters or pitchers to best fit their hitter or pitcher friendly ballparks. But it has already been mentioned that the speed and accuracy of pitchers does not differ whether home or away. And Moskowitz and Wertheim (2011) find that "Teams from hitters' ballparks outhit their visitors by the same amount as home teams in pitchers' parks do" and "teams that play at home in hitters' ballparks hit no better on the road than teams that play host in pitchers' ballparks do when they're on the road" (p. 133). So unique home field characteristics do not appear to play a role in home field advantage in baseball.

In football, playing conditions (such as due to weather) also differ from team to team. Do different teams recruit players to best fit their home environments and does that account for home field advantage? Moskowitz and Wertheim (2011) found that home field advantage does not differ for teams playing at home in one climate compared to playing away games in either the same or different climates. In addition, the physical playing conditions are virtually the same from venue to venue in many sports, such as basketball and hockey. But home field advantage still exists in those sports. So unique home field characteristics do not well account for home field advantage.

Scheduling. In some sports, such as the National Basketball Association (NBA) and the National Hockey League (NHL), away teams play more games on consecutive days, and more games within a shorter time period, than home teams. Such back-to-back games and the fatigue they produce does contribute to home team advantage. For example, differences in game schedules are responsible for about a fifth of the home field advantage in the NBA, according to Moskowitz and Wertheim (2011). In contrast, games are not played on consecutive days in the NFL and the effects of differential scheduling are not present, though home field advantage still is. Scheduling differences of a different sort can have large effects in college sports because, especially early in the season, the best teams often schedule inferior opponents for home games to enhance the home team records, and the away teams acquiesce because of financial payoffs and other incentives. The point is that scheduling accounts for a good proportion, but far from all, of the home field advantage.

Officiating. According to Moskowitz and Wertheim (2011) and their data, biases in officiating that favor the home team account for the lion's share of home field advantage. To support this conclusion, Moskowitz and Wertheim separated the effects of officiating from the effects of other factors. In so doing, Moskowitz and Wertheim found that officials (referees and umpires) affect some aspects of games free from the effects of other factors. Such aspects of games can be found, for example, in soccer where the head referee adds time to games because of delays that occur during the game. The data suggest that the head referee adds time to games so as to advantage the home team.

Or consider baseball where data show a bias in favor of the home team in that more balls and fewer strikes are called against home batters, where called balls and strikes determine strike outs and walks, and are decided by the head umpire. Interestingly, cameras were used in some stadiums to examine the accuracy of called balls and strikes. The home field bias in called balls and strikes was present when cameras were not used but disappeared when cameras were present and umpires knew they are being monitored for accuracy. The best explanation for such results is that umpires are biased in favor of home teams.

Professional football provides additional evidence of officiating bias. In the NFL, the home field advantage in turnovers called by officials diminished once instant replay was used to review calls because instant replay gives more opportunities for officiating bias to be detected and disciplined. But other differences in officiating between home and away teams, which instant replay would not affect, remained.

Officiating calls also favor home teams over away teams in professional basketball. The difference is greatest for officiating calls that require the most judgment by referees, which is what would be predicted if referee bias causes home field advantage. Similar results are found in professional hockey.

The point is that the data support the explanation that officiating is largely responsible for home field advantage. The reasons why officials are biased in favor of home teams is likely due to the influence of the home team fans who root loudly for the home team and loudly against the visiting team. Like most everyone else, officials want to please people more than they want to displease them. When confronted by a mass of vociferous fans, a bias in favor of the home team results.

Data are also in agreement with the conclusion that officiating bias is largely due to the influence of fans because of wanting to appease them. If the influence of fans is the cause of officiating bias, the greater the number of fans at the game and the closer the officials are to the fans, the greater should be the effect of the fans on the officials and therefore the larger should be home field advantage. Data are in agreement with both predictions.

Conclusions. The data Moskowitz and Wertheim (2011) present support the conclusion that home field advantage is largely due to biases in officiating wherein game officials favor the home team. And the data Moskowitz and Wertheim present are far more extensive than I have briefly summarized here. Moskowitz and Wertheim (2011) reach their conclusions using the multiple hypotheses method where different plausible hypotheses are assessed and some hypotheses are shown to outperform others in explaining the massive and multifaceted data they have accumulated. Of course, Moskowitz and Wertheim are not without their critics (Birnbaum, 2011; Brook, 2012), but the value of the multiple hypotheses method still stands.

The Connecticut Crackdown on Speeding

In an effort to reduce the number of traffic fatalities, which was at a record high in his state, Connecticut Governor Abraham Ribicoff instituted a crackdown on speeding at the end of 1955. By the conclusion of 1956, traffic fatalities had declined by 12 percent (from 324 in 1955 to 284 in 1956), which the Governor attributed to the effect of the crackdown. In a widely cited article, Campbell and Ross (1968) used the method of multiple hypotheses to assess whether that hypothesis was plausible (Campbell, 1969, 1970, 1972).

Before they were willing to credit the decrease in traffic fatalities to the crackdown on speeding, Campbell and Ross (1968) investigated six alternative explanations. First, the decrease in fatalities might be due to other, unrelated events that occurred in 1956. For example, perhaps the weather was different from year to year, with less snow in 1956 being responsible for the decrease in the number of fatalities. An effect due to such an event is said to be due to *history*. Second, people grow older over time and the decrease in fatalities could be due to the aging of the population from 1955 to 1956 because older drivers tend to drive more cautiously than younger drivers. Such an effect is said to be due to *maturation*. Third, knowledge of the record high death rate in 1955 (perhaps made known by media reports) might, by itself, have stimulated people to drive more carefully the next year. Such an effect is said to be due to *testing*. Fourth, a decrease in fatalities could have arisen if deaths were measured differently in 1955 than in 1956. Perhaps traffic fatalities were recorded in 1955 if the causes of death were attributed to traffic accidents either at the scene of the accident or at any time afterward, such as during hospitalization. In contrast, perhaps traffic fatalities were recorded in 1956 only if the victims were dead at the scene of the accident. If so, such a difference in *instrumentation* might have accounted for the decline in reported traffic fatalities. Fifth, a decline in traffic fatalities of 12 percent might be no more than is expected by random differences in fatalities from year to year. Such an effect is said to be due to *chance* or *instability*. Sixth, the decrease in traffic fatalities might have arisen because the number of fatalities in 1955 was extremely high and would therefore likely revert to a more typical, lower number in 1956. Such an effect is said to be due to *regression toward the mean* (Furby, 1973).

To choose among the seven possible explanations for the decline in traffic fatalities (i.e., the crackdown on speeding plus the six alternative hypotheses), Campbell and Ross (1968) examined additional data besides the data from one year before and one year after the crackdown. First, they added data from multiple years and multiple months both before 1955 and after 1956. And they added data from four states that are neighbors of Connecticut (namely, Massachusetts, New Jersey, New York, and Rhode Island). With such additional evidence in hand, the effects of history could be assessed by comparing the differences in fatalities from before to after 1955 across the different states. Assuming history effects (such as weather changes across years) affected all five states in much the same way, history could explain the results only if there were similar declines in fatalities from before 1955 to after 1955 in all the states and not just in Connecticut. Conversely, if there was no decline in fatalities in the neighboring states but there was a decline in Connecticut, a potential history effect shared by all the states would not be a plausible alternative explanation for the decline in Connecticut.

An alternative explanation for the 1955–1956 decline in fatalities in Connecticut due to maturation would be plausible only if a time-series of data from years before 1955 showed a downward trend in traffic fatalities before the crackdown. That no such downward trend was present means that maturation could not plausibly account for the decline in traffic fatalities in Connecticut from before to after 1955.

Fluctuations from year to year would allow a researcher to judge the likelihood that chance or instability could account for the decline in traffic fatalities from before to after 1955. Because the decline in fatalities from before to after 1955 was large compared to the other changes from year to year, chance was not a plausible explanation for the decline from 1955 to 1956.

Regression toward the mean would only be plausible as an explanation for the decline in fatalities from 1955 to 1956 if fatalities in 1955 were substantially greater than in preceding years, which was the case. Then it would be plausible to assume that a large decline in 1956 could simply be a return to a more typical number of fatalities. The likelihood that a decline was due to regression toward the mean was increased because the crackdown on speeding was implemented precisely because traffic accidents were so unusually numerous in 1955.

Finally, the effects of testing and instrumentation could be assessed with even more supplementary data, such as from newspaper reports and government record-keeping documents. For example, if a testing effect was due to publicizing the record number of traffic fatalities from 1955, a researcher might find that such publicity would be evident in newspaper articles.

In addition, an effect of a crackdown would be most plausible if, after 1955, there was both a decrease in the relative number of violations for speeding and an increase in the number of drivers' licenses that were suspended due to speeding. Such decreases and increases are analogous to manipulation checks in experimental research, whereby a researcher determines if the intervention under investigation was implemented with adequate fidelity, strength, and content to plausibly produce an observed effect (Kidd, 1976).

The extensive identification of both alternative hypotheses and relevant data by Campbell and Ross (1968) provides another example of the application of the method of multiple hypotheses. After examination of the data as predicted by the various hypotheses, Campbell and Ross (1968) concluded that effects due to either the crackdown on speeding or regression toward the mean, or both, remained plausible as explanations for the decline in traffic fatalities.

The alternative hypotheses Campbell and Ross (1968) describe and label (as given above) are well recognized both in writings on research methods and in research practice. Such alternative explanations are called threats to internal validity and are front and center, for example, in the seminal and widely influential methodological works of Campbell and Stanley (1966), Cook and Campbell (1979), and Shadish, Cook, and Campbell (2002). In taking account of threats to internal validity, as done by Campbell and Ross (1968), researchers are using the MH method.

More on Threats to Internal Validity

As just noted, threats to internal validity were addressed in the study by Campbell and Ross (1968) of the effects of the Connecticut crackdown on speeding. The threats to internal validity were alternative hypotheses for the reduction in traffic fatalities from 1955 to 1956. Although they were not labeled as such, threats to internal validity were also addressed in the other two studies by Levitt and Dubner (2005) and Moskowitz and Wertheim (2011).

Consider the Levitt and Dubner (2005) study of the causes of the decline in crime in the U.S. during the 1990s. Levitt and Dubner began by identifying various alternative hypotheses to consider as explanations for the decline in crime (e.g., improved economy, more use of capital punishment, stricter gun control laws, an aging population, and so on). For each of these potential causes, Levitt and Dubner used additional data to determine if the potential cause could plausibly account for any of the decline in crime. In so doing, comparisons were drawn in which threats to internal validity could arise. For example, one of the potential explanations for the decline in crime was that a greater number of police had been hired in cities across the U.S. in the 1990s. Additional data supported that alternative explanation as a partial cause of the decrease in crime. The data used were derived from a comparison between cities where police were added and cities where police were not added. But in some cities police were added in response to prior increases in crime so a greater number of police would be associated with an increase in crime, rather than a decrease. To avoid this threat to internal validity (called *selection differences*) in the comparison being drawn, Levitt and Dubner investigated only cities where police were not added in response to increasing crime. Comparisons using such cities showed that crime was reduced, rather than increased, by adding police. The point is that threats to internal validity arose as alternative hypotheses in Levitt and Dubner and were ruled out as plausible explanations for observed differences.

Also consider the Moskowitz and Wertheim (2011) study of the causes of home field advantage in sports. Moskowitz and Wertheim began by identifying various alternative hypotheses to consider as explanations for home field advantage (i.e., fans, travel, home field characteristics, scheduling, and officiating). For each of these potential causes, Moskowitz and Wertheim used additional data to determine if the potential cause could plausibly account for any of the home field advantage. In so doing, comparisons were drawn in which threats to internal validity could arise. For example, the primary explanation that Moskowitz and Wertheim hypothesized was that home field advantage was due, in large part, to biases in officiating. Data supported the hypothesis of officiating bias because it was shown that officials in basketball games called more fouls on visiting teams than on home teams. However, a threat to internal validity (called selection differences) arises in such a comparison between home and away teams because poor play on the part of the visiting team, rather than officiating bias, might account for the differences in the number of fouls called. That threat to internal validity was ruled out by finding differences in called fouls only when the calls were most ambiguous, which meant the calls involved the most judgment on the part of the officials. If poor play, rather than officiating bias, were the cause of differences in called fouls, the differences should appear even when the fouls did not involve judgment calls. The point is again that threats to internal validity arose as alternative hypotheses in Moskowitz and Wertheim and were ruled out as plausible explanations for observed differences.

Threats to internal validity are ubiquitous and usually arise when answering questions about cause and effect. Threats to internal validity are alternative explanations for observed differences and must be either ruled out or ruled in when drawing causal conclusions. Most textbooks on research methods in the social/behavioral sciences discuss threats to internal validity, especially in the context of quasi-experimental designs (Shadish, Cook, & Campbell, 2002; Reichardt, 2019). These textbooks usually go to some length to explain that threats to internal validity are rival hypotheses to the preferred explanation for the results of design comparisons. These textbooks usually emphasize that threats to internal validity must be taken into account before confident conclusions can be drawn about the preferred explanation for observed differences. In this way, the textbooks are employing the multiple hypothesis method, even if they do not provide a general description of the scientific method in those terms.

Summary

The three examples by Levitt and Dubner (2005), Moskowitz and Wertheim (2011), and Campbell and Ross (1968) well illustrate the use of the method of multiple hypotheses in both identifying and taking account of alternative hypotheses. In all three examples, the authors considered multiple hypotheses before reaching conclusions about which hypothesis or hypotheses among many were most plausible. Consideration of multiple alternative hypotheses is the hallmark of the MH method. In all cases, some of the alternative hypotheses include threats to internal validity. The authors could not have drawn conclusions as confidently, could not have produced as strong inferences, if the full range of alternative hypotheses had not been addressed. The MH method might not be as widely presented in the literature as the H-D method when defining the scientific method. But the MH method is nonetheless widely used in practice and widely taught in research methods texts in the context of ruling out threats to internal validity. The MH method is especially widely used in the most rigorous research, as in the examples in this chapter.

Chapter 5

Advantages of the Multiple Hypotheses Method

I have presented two methods for justifying beliefs about reality. Chapter 2 presented the hypothetico-deductive (H-D) method and noted that it is often described on websites and in the literature. Chapter 3 then presented the multiple hypotheses (MH) method and Chapter 4 gave examples of the MH method. The primary difference between the two methods is the following. As the H-D method is most often presented, a researcher using the H-D method studies a single hypothesis and need not consider alternative hypotheses to that hypothesis. As the H-D method is most often portrayed on the web and in the literature, the researcher chooses a hypothesis to study, derives one or more implications of the hypothesis, assesses the implication or implications, and draws a conclusion about the acceptability of the hypothesis. If, in using the H-D method, the data conform to the implication or implications of the hypothesis under investigation, the hypothesis is said to be corroborated, confirmed, accepted or something along those lines. For such a conclusion to be reached, a researcher using the H-D method need never have considered alternative hypotheses.

In contrast, the MH method makes the comparison of alternative hypotheses a central component of a decision to accept a hypothesis. The MH method forces the researcher to identify and place alternative hypotheses into a survival-of-the-fittest competition with the favored hypothesis. That a hypothesis conforms to the given data is not sufficient for accepting that hypothesis in the MH method. For a researcher using the MH method to accept a hypothesis, the data must conform to that hypothesis and must not conform nearly as well to any alternative hypotheses. Otherwise the researcher is not justified in choosing to accept one hypothesis over some other hypothesis that is just as well supported by the evidence.

Because the MH method focuses on alternative hypotheses while the H-D method does not, the MH method is more demanding than the H-D method. As a result, the H-D method is both easier to teach and put into practice than the MH method. However, because it ignores alternative hypotheses, the H-D method has several weaknesses compared to the MH method. The present chapter describes eight advantages of the MH method compared to the H-D method.

DOI: 10.4324/9781003198413-5

Identifying a Correct Hypothesis

There is no guarantee that any of the hypotheses investigators identify will be true. However, investigators can improve their chances of identifying a correct hypothesis by considering more than one. The more hypotheses investigators consider, the more likely it is that they will have the correct one, or at least have a hypothesis that is close to correct. Because the MH method emphasizes identifying multiple hypotheses right from the start, it is more likely than the H-D method to identify the correct, or close to correct, hypothesis right from the start. At its best, the H-D method considers alternative hypotheses only when the available data do not conform to the hypothesis currently under investigation. Even then, the H-D method considers alternatives only one at a time, one after the other. The MH method emphasizes the identification of all plausible alternative hypotheses in the very first step.

Abandoning Incorrect Hypotheses

People have a tendency to stop coming up with explanations once an initial explanatory hypothesis is identified (Nisbett & Ross, 1980). People are often quite willing and eager to provide a hypothesis to explain a phenomenon. Indeed, people are evolutionarily primed to find patterns and explain them. But people often stop with a single hypothesis or explanation. Once an explanation that seems to fit the available data has been identified, it goes against people's natural proclivity to provide further explanations. And once people have an explanation, people can become overly attached to it, confident it is the correct one, and lose sight of the possibility it could be incorrect. As Chamberlin (1890/1965) argues, researchers tend to become enamored of a hypothesis once they have identified it, especially if they consider it their own unique creation. Becoming enamored of a hypothesis can lead to confirmation bias wherein researchers seek data that only supports that one hypothesis and interpret data only to be in support of that one hypothesis (Lord, Ross, & Lepper, 1979). The MH method helps researchers resist such temptations. By having multiple hypotheses at hand right from the start, researchers would have less tendency to become emotionally attached to any one hypothesis and so have less tendency to suffer from confirmation biases and the resulting over confidence in favoring one hypothesis over others (Greenwald, Pratkanis, Leippe, & Baumgardner, 1986). And when data suggest that a hypothesis is implausible it may be easier for investigators to abandon it if they have not become overly attached to it. That researchers are less likely to become attached to a hypothesis using the MH method than using the H-D method is an advantage of the MH method.

Providing a True Sense of the Acceptability of a Hypothesis

Consider the case where two hypotheses, X and Y, are equally in agreement with the available evidence. Further suppose a researcher employing the H-D method had chosen to investigate hypothesis X, thereby ignoring hypothesis Y. Then the researcher could well obtain a false sense of the acceptability of hypothesis X, if the data collected were in agreement with hypothesis X. In that case, the H-D method would lead the researcher to accept hypothesis X without recognizing that hypothesis Y fits the available data equally well. In contrast, a researcher employing the MH method would not be able to accept hypothesis X. Unlike the H-D method, the MH method forces researchers to collect additional data to distinguish between the two hypotheses before judging belief in either to be justified.

For an example, consider the theory of intelligent design (ID), which is the theory that earthly species were created by a powerful intelligence rather than by evolution through natural selection. Because (at least some versions of) ID theory specify that each separate species was created simultaneously and discretely rather than through gradual evolution, those versions of ID theory predict gaps between species in the fossil record. Because innumerable gaps in the fossil record exist, those who believe in intelligent design can claim the existence of innumerable gaps supports their theory. And in accordance with the H-D model, the gaps do indeed lend credence to the theory of ID—the theory of ID predicts gaps, gaps are found, hence this evidence appears to justify belief in the theory of ID in accordance with the H-D model. Indeed, as I write this, a web site on intelligent design reports that ID theory is scientific precisely because support for it can be generated following the H-D method (https://intelligentdesign.org/whatisid).

What is missing in the H-D method is the realization that the existence of gaps adds just as much credence to the theory of evolution through natural selection as to ID theory. While the theory of evolution through natural selection predicts no significant gaps in transition forms between species, the theory nonetheless predicts gaps in the fossil record. Gaps in the fossil record exist because it is both rare for bones to become fossilized and for researchers to find the rare fossils. As a result, the fossil record is an imperfect reflection of the full range of species that have existed over the eons. Because gaps in the fossil record are predicted by both the theory of ID and the theory of evolution through natural selection, the gaps in no way distinguish between the two theories and hence should do little to lend credence to the theory of ID as compared to the theory of evolution through natural selection. That is, according to the MH method, gaps in the fossil record do not justify accepting the theory of ID because the data just as well support the theory of evolution through natural selection.

The same conclusion holds for the finding that species are well adapted to their environments. ID proponents can argue such adaptation is a consequence of the foresight and planning of an intelligent designer. But the theory of evolution through natural selection makes the same prediction that species will be well adapted to their environments. So species' adaptation to environments does not lend credence to the ID theory any more than to the theory of Darwinian evolution. Nonetheless, the H-D model can take the evidence of species' adaptation as justification for belief in the ID theory. In contrast, the MH method finds that species' adaptability is not grounds for accepting ID theory because that data does not distinguish between ID theory and the theory of evolution through natural selection.

The point is that the H-D model allows ID advocates to fool themselves, and perhaps others, into believing that the evidence of fossil gaps and species' adaptability means the theory of ID can be accepted. In contrast, because it considers alternative hypotheses, the MH method would not find that the data of fossil gaps or species' adaptability means ID theory can be accepted. By considering only a single hypothesis at a time, a false sense of the credence of that hypothesis can be obtained with the H-D method. The MH method requires a decision about the acceptance of a hypothesis be delayed until the evidence supports one hypothesis more than any other hypothesis. A hypothesis "is not to be received probably true because it accounts for all the known phenomena; since this is a condition sometimes fulfilled tolerably well by two conflicting hypotheses" (John Stuart Mill cited in the online *Stanford Encyclopedia of Philosophy*). That the MH method delays acceptance of a hypothesis until plausible alternative hypotheses are discredited is an advantage of the MH method over the H-D method.

Assessing Data Relevant to Alternative Hypotheses

As most often presented in the literature, the H-D method does not specify that a researcher continue to investigate a hypothesis once a set of data is found that agrees with the implications of the hypothesis. As the H-D method is presented most often, a researcher concludes a hypothesis is corroborated after a single implication of the hypothesis is found to hold true. Some descriptions of the H-D method specify the next step is to replicate the given findings of a research project. But it is the rare explicit description of the H-D method that specifies assessing additional implications once a hypothesis has been corroborated by agreement with the first implication assessed. In contrast, the MH method explicitly specifies that relevant evidence be diligently identified and assessed. This means the researcher is to identify and assess all relevant evidence. Certainly, the surest way to knowledge is to examine more, rather than less, relevant data. Hall and Johnson (1998) even go so far as to argue, in keeping with the logic of the MH method, that researchers have an epistemic duty to continually seek out additional data.

But even if a researcher were to investigate additional implications of a corroborated hypothesis using the H-D method, the MH method is a superior method for choosing the additional implications to investigate. By focusing on a competition among alternative hypotheses, the MH method emphasizes obtaining data that help distinguish among alternative hypotheses. "The evidence that might refute a theory can often be unearthed only with the help of an incompatible alternative" (Feyerabend, 1975, p. 29). Without any alternative hypotheses in mind, the H-D method could all too easily perseverate on using data that do not distinguish among plausible hypotheses and therefore do little to advance knowledge.

As an example consider, once again, a researcher who uses the H-D method to assess the theory of intelligent design. As noted before, an implication of the ID theory is that species A would be well suited to its environment. Following the H-D method a researcher could assess whether such a state of affairs was present. Then the researcher could assess whether species B was well suited to its environment. Then the researcher could study species C. And so on. In accordance with the H-D method, a sequence of positive results from such studies would add further and further credibility to the ID theory. In contrast, the MH method would recognize that such a series of studies would not add to the credibility of ID theory because the theory of evolution through natural selection predicts the same adaptability across species. As a result, the series of studies would do nothing to distinguish between the ID theory and the theory of evolution through natural selection. The point is the preceding program of research directed by the H-D method would not progress toward discovering the truth very quickly, if at all. In contrast, a program of research under the guise of the MH method would likely progress much more quickly because it would focus on obtaining data that distinguish between ID theory and the theory of evolution by natural selection. Which empirical implications best distinguish alternative hypotheses is a central concern in the MH method but not in the H-D method. The MH method guides the identification of implications and the diligent collection of data needed to hone in on the best hypothesis. The H-D method does not.

Importantly, the MH method is the method often used in sophisticated science when a new hypothesis is introduced that challenges an accepted hypothesis. Consider, for example, what happened when Einstein's theory of relativity was propounded as an alternative to Newtonian mechanics. In that case, researchers used the MH method to deduce consequences of Einstein's theory that conflicted with the consequences of Newton's theory. One of the most dramatic and immediately testable differences between the predictions of the two theories is that Einstein's theory specifies that light rays can bend significantly in the presence of sufficient gravity while Newton's theory does not make that prediction. And researchers were quick to propose and conduct a test of the effects of gravity on light. Einstein's theory won. In contrast, the H-D method would have allowed researchers to assess predictions of Einstein's theory whether or not they differed from predictions of Newtonian mechanics.

It might be argued that one way to fortify the H-D method would be to add the proviso, as Popper does (1965; Giere, 1998; Laudan, 1998b; Meehl, 1978), that the best tests of a hypothesis are tests of risky predictions, where a risky prediction foretells an outcome that would occur if the hypothesis were correct but would be unexpected to occur if the hypothesis were incorrect. Or another way to say the same thing is that a risky prediction is compatible with the hypothesis under study but contrary to what would appear to be most plausible to arise if the hypothesis were not true. Passing a test involving a highly risky prediction is said to provide stronger corroboration of a hypothesis than passing a test involving a less risky prediction. As Lakatos (1970, p. 27) puts it, assessing risky predictions of a hypothesis means the hypothesis is made to "stick its neck out." In this way, focusing on risky predictions strengthens tests of a solitary hypothesis, such as involved in the H-D method.

Note, however, that identifying the degree of riskiness of an implication requires specifying at least one alternative state of nature (i.e., what would likely be the case if the hypothesis under investigation were incorrect) which is in keeping with the MH method but not the H-D method. And note further that riskiness would be best assessed in the context of specific plausible alternative hypotheses. Indeed, what would be most risky for a hypothesis is a test of an implication that was at odds with the implications of all other plausible hypotheses. The point is that riskiness makes perfect sense within the framework of the MH method, perhaps even more so than within the framework of the H-D method. Indeed, focusing on riskiness follows naturally once the process of belief justification is conceptualized in terms of the MH method. The MH researcher naturally thinks in terms of implications that distinguish among alternative hypotheses, which are the riskiest of predictions according to Popperian logic.

Or think about it this way: What would seem most plausible to arise if a hypothesis were not true serves the function of alternative hypotheses to that hypothesis. That is, what would seem most plausible to arise if a hypothesis were not true can be a placeholder for the implications of alternative hypotheses that are currently unforeseen. Therefore, when using a risky prediction, a researcher puts a hypothesis into competition with as-yet-unidentified alternative hypotheses in the same way a researcher following the MH method would place the hypothesis into competition with explicit alternative explanations, were they available. Popper is correct to suggest the use of risky predictions. It's just that the use of risky predictions is justified by the logic of the MH method. Use risky predictions when implementing the H-D method. But a researcher is also using risky predictions when implementing the MH method to assess evidence that distinguishes among alternative hypotheses. And when alternative hypotheses have been identified, using risky predictions to choose between them means the investigator is using the MH method rather than the H-D method.

Retaining Hypotheses

According to most descriptions of the H-D method, the hypothesis under investigation must be either modified or rejected when the implications of that hypothesis do not conform to the obtained data. Continuing to entertain a hypothesis in the face of apparently conflicting evidence is generally not presented as an option in the H-D method. But Hempel (1966) and Lakatos (1968, 1970, 1978) long ago explained that common practice does not follow the H-D method's prescriptions. They argued that data inconsistent with a hypothesis neither should nor does lead to the rejection of a hypothesis unless and until a better hypothesis has been identified that is shown to be superior to a to-be-rejected hypothesis based on the evidence. Kuhn (1970) also noted that hypotheses that are central to a research program are not rejected during what he called normal science. During such periods of scientific activity, results that contradict a foundational hypothesis do not lead to the rejection of that hypothesis but are set aside as puzzles to be dealt with later.

Numerous examples well demonstrate that the wisest decision can often be to retain an unmodified hypothesis even in the face of apparently disconfirming data. The discovery of Neptune provides an example. When Uranus' orbit was first carefully plotted, it was found to deviate from the predictions of Newton's laws of motion. According to the H-D method, such a refutation would require either the modification or rejection of Newton's laws. Instead, scientists proposed that the gravitational pull of an as yet undiscovered planet was responsible for the deviations of Uranus from Newtonian expectation. Indeed, calculations based on Newton's laws suggested where to look to discover such a planet. And the planet of Neptune was found as expected. The point is, given the immense wealth of data to support Newton's laws, it made more sense to retain Newton's theories and seek to rectify apparently conflicting data in other ways than to reject or modify the well-established theory. As typically presented, the H-D method does not allow for such a course of action. Or consider the motion of the earth around the sun. A heliocentric system would be irrefutably dismissed under the H-D method, given the obvious sense data that the earth is still and it is the sun that moves. According to the MH method, a hypothesis can be retained even in the face of conflicting data, as long as no alternative hypothesis is judged superior.

Resurrecting Hypotheses

As most often described, the H-D method has no mechanism for resurrecting a hypothesis once it has been rejected or modified. According to the H-D methods, if a hypothesis is modified or rejected, the original hypothesis is apparently no longer in the running as a potential theoretical candidate. Yet numerous instances of the resurrection of hypotheses arise in practice. For example, as already noted, the theory of continental drift was originally roundly dismissed by the scientific community because, when first proposed, it was incompatible with available data and theory. Subsequently, when mechanisms for continental movement were discovered, the theory was resurrected and is now widely accepted. Permanent banishment seems to be the outcome of the H-D method but is not the case with the MH method.

In the MH method, a hypothesis can be rejected at one point in time in favor of a different hypothesis. But when the MH method rejects one hypothesis in favor of another, the spurned hypothesis need not be rejected permanently. With the MH method, hypotheses that are rejected at one point in time can later, when more data are diligently obtained, be resurrected because they are found to better explain the new data than can previously accepted hypotheses. Indeed, Feyerabend (1975) explicitly suggests that previously falsified theories continue to be pursued as rigorously as currently accepted hypotheses because unaccepted hypotheses might turn out to be true while it is the apparently falsifying data that are subsequently invalidated. The MH method is an iterative, never ending process of the diligent identification of hypotheses and data exploration which means no hypothesis need be permanently rejected and a previously unaccepted hypothesis can later be resurrected based on subsequent data. Being diligent in identifying hypotheses means constantly reconsidering all hypotheses even when they were previously rejected. Being diligent in identifying hypotheses means there is a possibility of reconsidering and resurrecting hypotheses, which is an option that can lead to significant advance in science. No such mechanisms are part of the H-D method.

Improving Critical Thinking Skills

Sophisticated researchers need to be able to think critically. Thinking critically includes identifying and investigating alternative explanations (Ennis, 1987). Researchers who follow the MH method learn these critical thinking skills. Researchers who learn the MH method become predisposed to asking how evidence can be explained in alternative ways and how investigations can be crafted to most clearly distinguish among alternative interpretations. Such predispositions are not emphasized or taught nearly as well when using the H-D method because that method does not focus on alternative explanations. Learning the MH method is likely to be an effective way to improve critical thinking and nurture appropriate skeptical attitudes. The MH method provides a better guide than the H-D method for learning how to think for oneself, as well as learning how to judge the veracity of what others think.

Demarcating Science from Pseudoscience

Physics is a classic science, at least in the way most academic physicists practice their craft. The same holds for chemistry, biology, economics, psychology, sociology and the rest of the natural and social/behavioral sciences. In contrast to science, consider pseudoscience. Classic examples of pseudoscience are astrology, biorhythms, geocentrism, graphology, homeopathy, intelligent design, iridology, numerology, therapeutic touch, and ufology, according to many. Pseudo means false or phony. Pseudoscience is considered a false or phony attempt at being scientific.

Scientists and philosophers of science have long been concerned with the manner in which science can be distinguished from pseudoscience. For example, the problem of demarcating science from pseudoscience was what helped prompt Popper (1965, 1968) to develop his well-known theory of falsification.

For Popper, a hypothesis is scientific if it is falsifiable and unscientific if it is not. For a hypothesis to be falsifiable, some potentially observable result must be capable of shedding doubt on the correctness of the hypothesis. Popper argued that some theories were not falsifiable because they was so double jointed they could account for any possible empirical result. In such instances, no result is incompatible with a theory so no data could encourage those who believe in that theory to alter their beliefs. According to Popper, theories that are unfalsifiable are pseudoscientific rather than scientific.

Alternative criteria for demarcation between science and pseudoscience are also possible (Laudan, 1998a; Thagard, 1998). The criterion I prefer is the following. Rather than demarcating science from pseudoscience based on the nature of their theories or hypotheses, science is best distinguished from pseudoscience based on their respective methods. This proposal is in keeping with a popular way to define science which is in terms of its methods of investigation rather than the substance of its empirical hypotheses. That is, what makes something a science is not so much the knowledge it has produced (i.e., its ontology) as the approach that is taken to acquiring knowledge (i.e., its epistemology). From this view, science is as much, if not more, a process as a product. As Sagan (1979) explained: "Science is a way of thinking much more than it is a body of knowledge" (p. 13). The point is that pseudoscience is to be distinguished from science because of the differences in their methods of investigation. The traditional sciences are scientific because they use the methods of scientific inquiry while pseudosciences are pseudoscientific because they do not use the scientific method, which is the MH method (Hines, 2003; Lilienfeld, Lohr, & Morier, 2001; Ruscio, 2006).

In pseudoscience few, if any, attempts are made to (a) thoroughly examine alternative hypotheses, (b) consider all the evidence relevant to plausible hypotheses, and (c) remain skeptical and tentative in the resulting conclusions. Pseudoscience considers only the one unquestioned hypothesis it prefers and gives short shrift to alternative hypotheses. Even then, pseudoscience does not consider all the evidence relevant to its favored hypotheses. Rather pseudoscience focuses only on evidence that supports its preferred hypothesis and ignores evidence that does not support that hypothesis—a practice known as cherry picking. For example, purported psychics can support their claims at least in part when they ignore how often their predictions fail and pay attention only to their successes. In addition, pseudoscience uses its cherry picked results to reach the conclusion that its favored pseudoscientific beliefs are correct without hesitation or doubt. And pseudoscientists don't change their views in the face of compelling data that refute their claims. For example, Kitcher (1995) notes that, while proponents of the pseudoscience called creation science claim evolution through natural selection is disproved by the second law of thermodynamics, such proponents have not changed their position in spite of compelling rebuttals of that critique. Instead, proponents of creation science "continue to present their ideas in exactly the same ways" in spite of countervailing evidence (Kitcher, 1995, p. 196). These are all unscientific approaches to inquiry.

In contrast, well-conducted science is not committed to a pre-specified hypothesis regardless of the evidence. Well-conducted science does not consider only cherry picked data and only interpretations of those data that lend support to its hypotheses. And well-conducted science is never certain in its conclusions. Pseudoscience selects data to fit its preordained hypotheses while well-conducted science fits its never certain hypotheses to data.

For present purposes, the point is not just that pseudoscience pursues non-scientific courses of action but also that the MH method does a better job than the H-D method of distinguishing between science and pseudoscience in these ways. The MH method makes clear, much more than does the H-D method, that investigators must be diligent in examining all plausible hypotheses, must use diligently collected evidence (which means all the data), must be willing to adjust their views in the face of disagreeable data, and must remain tentative in their conclusions. The H-D method does not insist that researchers diligently assess the myriad of possible implications nor put alternative hypotheses into competition. As seen with the examples from Intelligent Design, results supporting this pseudoscience can be said to be obtained in accord with the H-D method but not with the MH method. That is, the gaps in the fossil record and the adaptability of species can be said to provide confirmation of ID theory via the H-D method. In contrast, the MH method would make it abundantly clear that cherry picked evidence of fossil gaps and species' adaptability could not lead to the acceptance of ID theory because the evidence equally well supports Darwinian theory, so this evidence alone does not allow an intellectually honest researcher to accept one of the two theories any more or less than the researcher can accept the other.

Proponents of ID often want ID theory to be presented in the classroom on equal footing with the scientifically accepted theory of evolution through natural evolution and scientists have long fought to prevent ID theory from entering the classroom as accepted science. Scientists are correct in this battle because ID theory is pseudoscience and so should not be taught as if it were a legitimately accepted scientific theory. But perhaps ID theory could be brought into the classroom under a different guise, with beneficial effect. If ID theory were presented in the classroom not as a scientifically acceptable alternative to the theory of evolution through natural selection but as an alternative hypothesis that loses in a fair competition with natural evolution (when *all* the available evidence is considered) and if it were shown why ID theory fails to pass scientific muster in this competition, perhaps the credibility of ID theory would be diminished, at least among some of the unwary. In other words, rather than purging ID theory from the classroom which serves only to hide its flaws and to make proponents of ID theory charge that scientists conspire against ID theory, bringing ID theory into the classroom might provide a better way to reveal its flaws. And bringing ID theory into the classroom to reveal its flaws would be best accomplished using the MH method of belief justification.

As noted, the MH method explicitly reveals that science involves a competition among alternative hypotheses using all available data. In a direct competition between ID theory and the theory of evolution through natural selection using all the data, ID theory clearly loses. In contrast, the H-D method does not explicitly present science as a competition among alternative hypotheses. As just noted, the H-D method can all too easily be used to marshal evidence (such as gaps in the fossil record and that species are well adapted to their environments) to support ID theory. And without engaging ID theory in a direct competition with the theory of evolution through natural selection, that supporting evidence might allow ID theory to appear to be plausible. Perhaps ID proponents would not be so eager to bring ID into the science classroom, and scientists would not have to fight so hard to keep ID as accepted science out of the classroom, if it were recognized that, using the MH method, ID theory would be placed into, and soundly defeated in, a complete and fair competition with the theory of evolution through natural selection.

Investigations of other pseudosciences are akin to investigations of ID theory in that they are often conducted by researchers who adopt the H-D method of investigation more than the MH method. Such researchers often find evidence for outcomes that are predicted by a pseudoscientific hypothesis. Then, following the H-D method, these researchers conclude the evidence confirms the pseudoscientific hypothesis. But these researchers fail to acknowledge that the same evidence could be explained equally well in non-pseudoscientific ways and so the available evidence, in fact, provides no reason to accept the pseudoscientific beliefs any more than to accept alternative beliefs. Carl Sagan's (1979) famous exhortation that "extraordinary claims require extraordinary evidence" is simply a succinct way of stating that extraordinary claims require evidence that cannot plausibly be interpreted in alternative ways. In keeping with Sagan's slogan, the MH method focuses on evaluating alternative hypotheses. In contrast, the H-D method does not. As a result, the MH method does a better job than the H-D method in putting the lie to the misleading conclusions often drawn based on shoddy pseudoscientific investigations.

Why the H-D Method Remains so Prevalent in the Literature

As has already been noted, in spite of the many advantages of the MH method compared to the H-D method, the H-D method is very often presented in the literature as if it were the scientific method. In addition, in my experience, few students can well articulate the MH method when asked to explain how to justify a belief about nature. Instead students (and faculty) most often give a version of the H-D method, if they provide any answer at all.

Tradition and simplicity are likely some of the reasons why the H-D method is more commonly depicted in the literature and more frequently espoused than is the MH method. But there could be another reason as well. Part of the reason for the common failure to recognize the MH method might be the same reason for blindness to the gorilla in the famous studies by Simons and Chabris (1999) on selective attention. Participants in the Simons and Chabris studies watch a video in which people weave in and out among themselves while passing a basketball. The participants in the study are asked to count the number of times the people in the video pass the basketball among themselves. While busy watching the video and counting basketball passes, a substantial number of participants fail to notice that a woman wearing a gorilla suit strolls prominently across the screen. The reason the gorilla is overlooked, of course, is that the participants are too busy focusing their attention on the assigned task of counting basketball passes to notice much of anything else.

A parallel selective focus of attention may be taking place in understanding how to justify a belief about reality. The purpose of justifying a belief is to determine what is true. If asked how we know hypothesis X is true, our responses often focus attention selectively on hypothesis X and fail to focus attention on alternatives to hypothesis X. Why? Because it is not immediately obvious that alternative hypotheses are relevant to the task of assessing hypothesis X. To believe in hypothesis X about nature, it is obvious that a researcher needs to obtain empirical data that are relevant to hypothesis X. But it is not obvious that researchers also need to obtain empirical data relevant to alternative hypotheses. Focusing on counting basketball passes is equivalent to focusing on assessing data relevant to hypothesis X, while noticing the woman in the gorilla suit is equivalent to recognizing the importance of identifying and assessing data relevant to alternatives to hypothesis X. The gorilla is easy to see once participants in the study know it is present. The importance of identifying and assessing alternative hypotheses is also easy to appreciate once it receives attention. But many, if not most, observers have to be told about the gorilla if they are to see it.

Summary

The MH method has numerous advantages compared to the H-D method as a way of learning about nature. Nonetheless, descriptions of the H-D method are more prevalent in the literature and on the web than are descriptions of the MH method. As a result, researchers tend to be taught the H-D method, rather than the MH method, is the scientific way of knowing. But researchers need to be taught and to appreciate the MH method if they are to be efficient and effective investigators. A number of advantages will accrue if the MH method were taught and practiced rather than the H-D method.

It can be difficult for researchers to accept the MH method because it can seem complex compared to the H-D method. It can be hard to accept the idea that a researcher must entertain alternative hypotheses to hypothesis X when attention seems to be best focused solely on whether evidence agrees with hypothesis X. Nonetheless, it is the competition of alternative hypotheses in a survival-of-the-fittest battle, as specified in the MH method that is the best approach to justifying beliefs about reality. Rather than the H-D method, the MH method is what researchers need to be taught so they can understand the role played by alternative hypotheses and their implications, and so they can produce strong inferences about the state of nature.

Chapter 6

The Problem of Confirmation

I have presented the multiple hypotheses method as a way to learn about the world. Indeed, I believe the MH method of belief justification is clearly the best way to learn about the world. But researchers must be careful to understand what can and cannot be accomplished when using the MH method. This chapter explores one limitation of the MH method.

The limitation is that the MH method cannot be used to prove a hypothesis about reality is true. Indeed, there is no way, whether using the MH method of belief justification or any other method, to prove a hypothesis about reality is true. Perhaps this statement about the impossibility of proving a hypothesis is true will come as a surprise to some readers. So let me defend this statement in some detail. To make my claim as believable as possible, I will present six reasons to accept it.

Reason #1: The Underdetermination of Theory by Observation

To prove that a given hypothesis (hypothesis X) about reality is correct based on empirical evidence, a person must be able to show that no alternative hypothesis (e.g., hypothesis Y) could explain the same evidence that hypothesis X can explain. If hypothesis Y could explain all the same data as hypothesis X can explain, a researcher simply has not well shown that hypothesis X, rather than alternative hypothesis Y, should be accepted. Yet there is always more than one hypothesis that can explain all the available data. Indeed, as noted in Chapter 3, there is always an infinite number of alternative hypotheses that can explain any finite amount of data. This is not a controversial position and I'm not the only one espousing it. Weaver (1967), for one of many, concurs:

> It is widely recognized that any natural event has a number of possible explanations. It has been demonstrated that if a certain body of experience can be usefully interpreted through one particular theory, then there is always, in fact, an infinite number of other theories each of which will equally well accommodate the same body of experience.
>
> (p. 48)

DOI: 10.4324/9781003198413-6

The point is the following. It is impossible to prove a hypothesis about nature is true because alternative hypotheses always exist that can explain all the available data. The same conclusion can be stated in a variety of ways. No available evidence is sufficient to decide authoritatively among alternative hypotheses. No finite amount of data uniquely determines a hypothesis. And if there are alternative hypotheses that can explain all the data, researchers are not entitled to anoint just one as the single acceptable hypothesis. "Scientists are never entitled to believe a theory true because, however much supporting evidence that theory enjoys, there must exist competing theories, generated or not, that would be as well supported by the same evidence" (Lipton, 2004, p. 152). In the philosophy of science literature, the fact there are always alternative hypotheses that can explain any set of data is called the problem of the underdetermination of theory by observation.

I reached the same conclusion in Chapter 3 when noting that any body of evidence could always be interpreted as various combinations of dream and hallucination. A classic analogy can also be used to make the same point. The classic illustration of the underdetermination of theory by observation involves fitting lines to a set of points in a two-dimensional space. Consider a set of points that all fall on a straight line. Because the points all fall on a straight line, a straight line provides an adequate fit to these data. But there are many curved lines that could also fit the observed points. That is, a wide variety of curved lines, if they are each sufficiently wavy, can all pass through each of the points in the collection and therefore all perfectly fit all the points. If additional points are added to the graph that all fall on the straight line, some of the curved lines might no longer fit all the points. But many curved lines (indeed, an infinite number) could still be added that do fit all the points. No matter how many finite points are added, even if they all fall along a straight line, there will always be an infinite number of curved lines that also fit (i.e., pass through) all the points. This example illustrates the underdetermination of theory by observation if we interpret the points as equivalent to data and the lines (both straight and curved) as equivalent to hypotheses that can explain the data. The conclusion is that no matter how much data are available, they can always be explained by innumerable hypotheses even if they have to be more convoluted and less straightforward than a simple (i.e., straight-line) hypothesis. Researchers will never have more than a finite body of evidence and so they will never be able to rule out all alternative hypotheses so as to prove that only one is correct.

Now please do not misunderstand. I am not arguing that all hypotheses are equally plausible. If a large amount of data can be fit with a straight line, that hypothesis may be far more plausible than any other. But plausibility is not the same thing as proof. We can perhaps show that some hypotheses are more plausible than others, but we cannot prove that any one hypothesis is true and all the others are false based on any finite amount of data. To repeat, it is impossible to *prove* any given hypothesis is correct using observations because the observations can always be explained by alternative hypotheses instead. Alternative hypotheses will remain at least logical possibilities even if all these alternative hypotheses are exceedingly farfetched. But as long as alternative hypotheses are logically possible, you will not have proven that a preferred hypothesis is correct.

Reason #2: Examples of Tooth Fairies and Desks

Reason #1 illustrated the underdetermination of theory by observation using an analogy. The analogy used lines to represent hypotheses and points to represent data. It is possible to provide more substantive illustrations. Consider the case of the tooth fairy as told by Hall (2006). Hall hypothesizes that a tooth fairy does not exist and provides reasons for that hypothesis. But Hall can provide as much data as she likes to demonstrate a tooth fairy does not exist without being able to definitively rule out the alternative hypothesis that a tooth fairy does exist. If someone is sufficiently persistent they can always reinterpret any and all data to be in agreement with the alternative hypothesis that a tooth fairy exists. Here is how Hall illustrates the predicament.

Imagine a younger brother who believes in the tooth fairy and an older sister who is trying to disabuse her sibling of that belief. According to the brother, there is ample reason to believe a tooth fairy exists. For example, his parents told him about the tooth fairy and money indeed appears after he puts a lost tooth under his pillow, just as predicted if there were a tooth fairy. To counter this reasoning, the older sister provides extensive empirical evidence to demonstrate that a tooth fairy doesn't exist: children ultimately stop believing in the tooth fairy, money appears only when parents know about a lost tooth, a video camera reveals no tooth fairy at night, the money has the parent's fingerprints, missing teeth are in the possession of the parents, and the parents now affirm they are responsible for the money. But all of this evidence can be explained by the brother without denying the existence of a tooth fairy: the tooth fairy only comes to those who believe in her and only when her existence is not being challenged, the parents' fingerprints are on the money because the tooth fairy gets the money from the parents, the parents collect the teeth from the tooth fairy, and the parents are now covering up the truth. Any other data suggesting the tooth fairy does not exist could be explained in alternative ways as well.

The point, of course, is not that it is plausible to believe in the tooth fairy. I very strongly believe a tooth fairy is imaginary. It is highly plausible a tooth fairy is fictional. I would place a very large bet that a tooth fairy is not real. But no one can prove a tooth fairy is not real based on empirical observations because any data can always be interpreted in a way that is consistent with the existence of a tooth fairy. Of course, the interpretations may get more and more convoluted and far-fetched as more and more data are added to the mix, as happens in the tooth fairy example given in the preceding paragraph. But as long as the available data can possibly be reinterpreted in support of a tooth fairy, the existence of a tooth fairy has not been definitively denied based on the observed data.

Now take the opposite case where the most plausible argument is that something does, rather than does not, exist. When discussing the topic of proof in a classroom, I will point to a desk and declare that its existence cannot be proven based on empirical observation. I start with visual data that suggests there is a desk in front of us. But instead of a desk, there could be a holographic image which would explain the visual observation. Then I note that we can touch the apparent desk so as to feel its presence, something that would not be the case were the apparent desk no more than a holographic image. But to explain the sense of touch, I could postulate a force field accompanies the holographic image which would explain why a person can feel the apparent desk. Then I tap the apparent desk to produce a sound. But the sound could come from audio speakers located around the room so as to project a sound to the location of the fake desk. My students could then look for the speakers but I could insist that they are very small and inconspicuous—they appear just like a wall. Someone could note that holographic images, force fields, and speakers require electricity and suggest we turn off the power to the building which would make a fake desk disappear. But I could suggest there is an independent electrical generator, run on an alternative source of fuel, located in the basement. And so on. And I have not even invoked the idea that the observations from the hypothetical desk could all be explained as coming from a dream or from a computer that has control of our brain so as to make our senses tell us whatever the computer desires, as in *Matrix*-like or brain-in-a-vat explanations.

Again, please don't get me wrong. When I point to a desk in my classroom, I believe there is a desk there. And I am highly confident. I would bet a great deal of money on the existence of a desk based on the available evidence. But I cannot prove that a desk is present based on the available evidence. The reason for the inability to prove a desk is present is that there are always alternative hypotheses possible that can explain any evidence I can present, even if the alternative hypotheses are highly implausible. That is, no matter what data are presented I can always reinterpret them in alternative ways. That means it is impossible to prove the desk exists, given empirical observations.

Reason #3: Affirming the Consequent

Another classic way to demonstrate the impossibility of proving that a hypothesis about nature is correct is to examine the structure of an apparently logical argument that is presented as if it does prove a hypothesis is correct. Here is how that logical argument would go:

- i If hypothesis H is true, then consequence C must be true.
- ii We observe nature and find that consequence C is true.
- iii Therefore, hypothesis H is true.

Such reasoning may appear on the surface to prove hypothesis H is true. But such reasoning is fallacious. The error in such an argument is called the fallacy of affirming the consequent. It is easy to show why this form of argument is invalid. Here is an example:

i If it is raining (H), it must be cloudy (C).
ii It is cloudy (C).
iii Therefore it must be raining (H).

The argument about rain has the same logical structure as in the preceding argument about hypothesis H. But clearly the argument about rain is invalid. The premise of the argument (i.e., if it is raining, it must be cloudy) might well be true. But even if it has been demonstrated that it is cloudy, that in no way proves it is raining. In fact, it is often cloudy and not raining. The point is that the preceding argument cannot be used to prove that a hypothesis is correct. And no other form of logical argument has ever been found that could be used to prove a hypothesis is correct.

Another way to demonstrate the fallacy of affirming the consequent is to provide an explicit alternative explanation for the available evidence. Consider the following example from Campbell (1988d).

i Newton's theory of gravity predicts that the tides repeat in a specifiable pattern because of the gravitational pull of the moon, cannon balls have a certain flight when fired at a given angle and velocity, and the planets follow a certain route in the sky.
ii Observations show that all three of these predictions hold true.
iii Therefore, Newton's theory of gravity is correct.

The problem, of course, is that Einstein's theory of relativity makes the same predictions as given above (about tides, cannon balls, and planets) and Einstein's theory might be correct rather than Newton's theory. So the observations have not proven that Newton's theory is correct. The preceding argument is another example of the underdetermination of theory by observation.

Reason #4: The Inadequacy of Induction

Inferences about reality are sometimes drawn using induction. There are several forms of induction. All have the same weaknesses when it comes to using them to prove that a statement about reality is true. Consider just a couple of simple examples of induction. First, a large number of swans are observed and they are found to all be white. As a result, a researcher concludes that all swans are white. Second, the sun has always arisen in the past. Therefore, it will always arise in the future. These are inductive arguments. The argument from induction is that induction could be used to justify belief in a hypothesis: Numerous data support a hypothesis, therefore all data support the hypothesis which means the hypothesis must be correct.

Hume (1778) is often credited as the first to argue that induction is not logically justified. The problem is that some black swans have actually been found to exist. And at some point in time the sun will die as a star destroying the earth and so will not rise above the earth's horizon. Just because some evidence, even a large amount of evidence, supports a hypothesis does not mean the hypothesis is true.

Reason #5: Feeling Certain is Not the Same as Proof

Some people believe that feeling absolutely certain a hypothesis is correct proves the hypothesis is correct. But different people can feel absolutely certain about opposing and incompatible beliefs where the two beliefs cannot both be correct. Some people feel certain ghosts exist. Other people feel certain ghosts do not exist. Both cannot be right. Some people feel certain an alien spacecraft landed at Roswell, New Mexico in 1947 and that the government has tried to cover-up that fact. Other people feel certain an alien spacecraft did not land at Roswell and, therefore, there has been no government cover-up. Both sets of beliefs cannot be correct. Some people feel certain astrology is a valid way of understanding the world while others feel certain astrology is bogus. Both beliefs cannot be correct. Hence feeling certain about a hypothesis does not prove the hypothesis is correct, otherwise it would mean contradictory hypotheses are both correct, which is logically impossible.

Proving a hypothesis is true is different than being highly confident the hypothesis is true. Even if I felt absolutely certain that a hypothesis about the world is true, I can always be wrong. So a feeling of certainty does not prove that a statement about the world is correct. To prove a statement about nature is correct based on data, there must be no alternative way to interpret the data. Yet there always is at least one alternative interpretation for any data, if not infinitely many.

Reason #6: Mathematical Proofs Do Not Apply

But wait you might say. Are not mathematicians able to prove that statements are true? The answer is yes. So doesn't this mean mathematicians can prove hypotheses about nature are true? The answer is no.

Consider a mathematical proof that the angles in a triangle add up to 180 degrees. Draw two dashed, parallel lines as in Figure 6.1. Then draw a triangle between the two parallel lines as depicted by the solid lines in the figure. The angles in the triangle are labeled 1, 2, and 3. Based on Euclidean geometry, the angles labeled 1, 2, and 3 that make up the triangle can be proven to add up to 180 degrees. For this proof, note that the angles labeled 2 and 4 are alternate interior angles. According to Euclidean geometry, alternate interior angles have the same size. Similarly, angles 3 and 5 are alternate interior angles and, therefore, are equal. So the sum of angles 1, 2, and 3 is equal to the sum of angles 1,

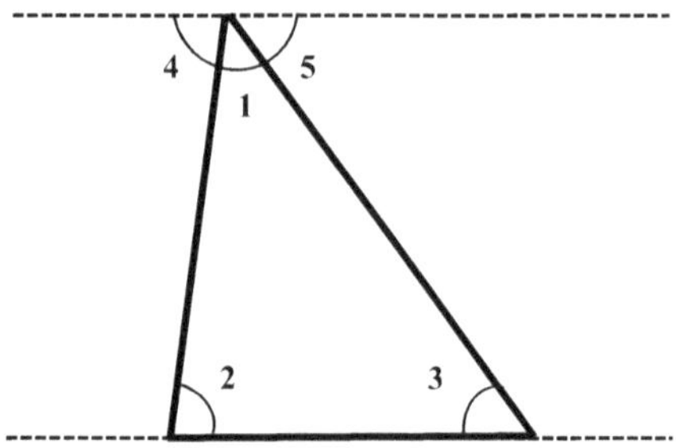

Figure 6.1 Proof the angles in a triangle add up to 180 degrees

4, and 5. Now notice how angles 1, 4, and 5 appear together along the top line. That these three angles span a straight line means these three angles add up to 180 degrees. Because the three angles in the triangle are equal to the three angles that span a straight line, the three angles that make up the triangle also add up to 180 degrees.

I have now apparently proved something about triangles as they exist in nature demonstrating, apparently, that mathematics can be used to prove a statement about nature is correct. But if this proof is examined carefully, it can be seen the proof rests on the assumptions of Euclidean geometry (e.g., that alternate interior angles are equal). The point is the following. That the three angles in a triangle add up to 180 degrees has been proven but only if the assumptions of Euclidean geometry are correct. In fact, the argument can be, and has been plausibly, made that nature is non-Euclidean. For example, Einstein's theory of relatively is based on non-Euclidean geometry because it assumes nature is curved. In non-Euclidean geometry, alternative interior angles are not equal. So if nature is non-Euclidean, I have not proved the angles in triangles add up to 180 degrees in nature. Because nature might not be Euclidean, I have not proved anything about nature. The same holds for all mathematical proofs.

A proof in mathematics takes the following form. Assumptions are first made (such as that Euclidean geometry holds true). Then consequences of those assumptions are deduced following the rules of logic. In this way, the logical implications of the assumptions are proven to be true if the assumptions hold true. But the assumptions have not been proven to be true. The assumptions are simply assumed to be true. If the assumptions are false, the consequences might be false. Mathematics is perfectly satisfied with such outcomes. Science is not.

Science is not satisfied with just deducing consequences of assumptions. Science wants to know if a hypothesis about nature is true whether or not a set of assumptions is true. Science wants to know if the angles in a triangle add up to 180 degrees whether or not Euclidean geometry is true. Mathematics does not answer such questions. Making assumptions and deriving consequences produces a mathematical proof but does not prove anything about nature. "As far as the propositions of mathematics refer to reality they are not certain; and as far as they are certain they do not refer to reality" (Einstein, 1922, p. 15).

If the nature of a proof in mathematics, or logic more generally, is examined, it will be seen that a proof does not provide any information that is not already contained in the assumptions. The information contained in the assumptions might not have been recognized before and might not be easily recognized. But all that mathematics or logic does is derive the consequences of assumptions. In contrast, the purpose of science is to gain knowledge beyond what is contained in assumptions.

Summary

It is impossible to prove that a hypothesis about reality is true. No matter how much evidence is available and no matter how plausible a hypothesis appears to be, the hypothesis can never be proven to be correct because whatever evidence is available can always be interpreted in alternative ways. That evidence can always be interpreted in multiple ways is called the underdetermination of theory by observation. That evidence can always be interpreted in multiple ways means that no one theory can ever be proven to be true based on data. Nor does any logical argument exist that can prove a hypothesis is correct. An argument that might appear to prove a hypothesis is correct is called affirming the consequent. However, affirming the consequent is logically fallacious. Nor do mathematical proofs provide a means to prove a statement about reality is true. Mathematical proofs are based on underlying assumptions, which might not be correct. As a result, any deductions derived from the proof might not correspond to reality.

If researchers are to draw conclusions about reality, they must be satisfied with a criterion other than proof. The present chapter lays the foundation for Chapter 8 wherein I argue the primary criterion to use in science (and in knowledge generation in general) is plausibility rather than proof. Plausibility is fallible. Researchers can always be wrong in their conclusions about reality. But plausibility is all researchers have to go on, rather than proof. And the MH method of warranting a claim to knowledge about nature can work well based on plausibility rather than proof.

Chapter 7

The Problem of Disconfirmation

The preceding chapter demonstrated that a hypothesis about nature cannot be proven to be true. As noted in that chapter, the conclusion that it is impossible to prove a hypothesis about nature is true is widely accepted. But what about disproving a hypothesis? Isn't that possible? It turns out the answer is no. It is not possible to either prove or disprove a hypothesis about nature. The purpose of the present chapter is to explain why disproof of a hypothesis about nature is impossible.

Many authors write as if it were possible to disprove hypotheses. Albert Einstein is often credited, with approval, as having said: "No amount of experimentation can ever prove me right; a single experiment can prove me wrong." Feynman (1965) argued that if a proposed law "disagrees with experiment it is wrong. That is all there is to it" (p. 156). And Popper (1965, 1968) proposed a falsificationist strategy wherein researchers could disconfirm a hypotheses about nature by showing its implications disagreed with observation.

Both Einstein and Feynman, in the preceding quotations, are wrong. A hypothesis or law is not necessarily wrong if it disagrees with experiential evidence. And Popper (1965, 1968) was not a naïve falsificationist. He knew that hypotheses could not be conclusively disproven. Data could shed doubt on a hypothesis but could not decisively prove it to be wrong. Popper (1968) stated this position forthrightly:

> no conclusive disproof of a theory can ever be produced; for it is always possible to say the experimental results are not reliable, or that the discrepancies which are asserted to exist between the experimental results and the theory are only apparent and that they will disappear with the advance of our understanding.
>
> (p. 50)

Deductive Argument: Denying the Consequent

One reason why so many people believe hypotheses about nature can be disproven is that a deductive argument is available that appears to provide

DOI: 10.4324/9781003198413-7

disproof. That is, disproof appears to proceed according to a valid deductive argument. The deductive argument is the following.

i If hypothesis H is true, then consequence C must be true.
ii We observe nature and find that consequence C is not true.
iii Therefore, hypothesis H is not true.

The above argument has the following abstract logical form:

i If H, then C.
ii C is not true.
iii Therefore, H is not true.

This is a valid logical argument called equivalently modus tollens or denying the consequent. Because this is a logically valid argument and because the conclusion is that the hypothesis is false, the argument appears to provide a means of falsifying a hypothesis conclusively.

But looks can be deceiving. One problem lies with step i. If step i cannot be implemented, the conclusion in step iii cannot be drawn. The problem is that step i cannot be implemented as stated. It is not possible, in step i, to deduce consequence C from hypothesis H without additional assumptions—called auxiliary assumptions. As a result, it is not possible to disprove a hypothesis using the modus tollens argument given above because the disproof requires assumptions, and it could be the assumptions, rather than the hypothesis under investigation, that are wrong.

As an example, consider an apparent disproof that the earth is flat. First, consider the state of affairs if the earth is round. If the earth is round, observers could not see the surface of the earth past a horizon in the distance. Even aboard an airplane above the earth's surface, the line of sight would reach only so far along the surface of the earth, as depicted in Figure 7.1, in which the solid, curved line represents the round earth and the dashed line represents the line of sight. A horizon would appear where the line of sight from the airplane

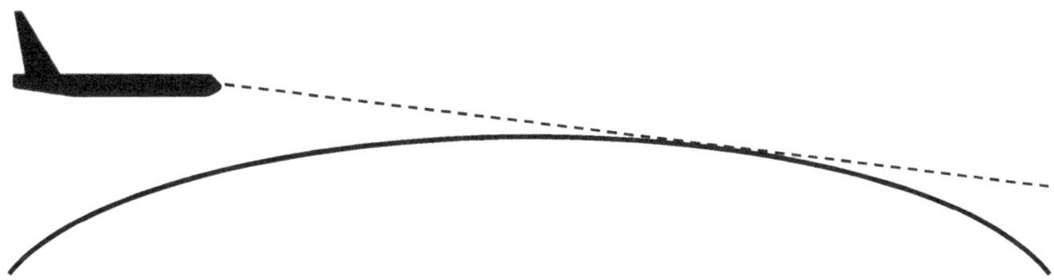

Figure 7.1 If the earth were round, the earth's surface would not be visible beyond the horizon

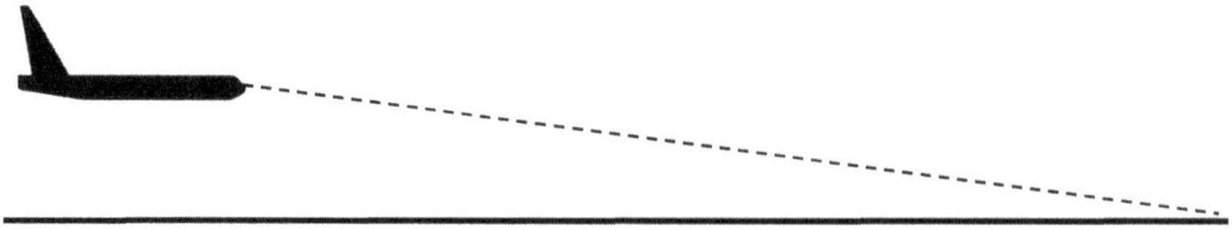

Figure 7.2 If the earth were flat, observers could see to the ends of the earth

in Figure 7.1 touches the earth. Beyond that horizon, the line of sight would rise above the surface of the earth. Nothing on the surface of the earth beyond that horizon would be visible from the plane.

In contrast, consider if the earth were flat as depicted by the flat solid line in Figure 7.2. Here the line of sight from an airplane, as represented by the dashed line, reaches to the end of the earth. There would be no horizon beyond which the surface of the earth would be shielded from view. Based on these two, conflicting implications of the earth being round or flat, it would seem an observer from an airplane could disprove that the earth is flat. A flat earth implies having a line of sight all the way to the end of the earth. Not having a line of sight all the way to the end of the earth would disprove a flat earth. Upon observing from inside an airplane, it will be found that there is no line of sight to the end of the earth. So the earth cannot be flat. QED.

But note that the preceding implications about lines of sight assume that light travels in straight lines as in Figures 7.1 and 7.2. If light were to bend rather than travel in straight lines, the implications would be different, were the earth to be flat (Copi, 1978). In particular, if the path of light were curved, as depicted by the curved, dashed line in Figure 7.3, an observer in a plane would see a horizon, even if the earth were flat. That is, if the earth were flat but the path of light were curved, the line of sight from an airplane would reach only so far alone the surface of the earth. A horizon would appear where the line of sight from the airplane in Figure 7.3 touches the earth. Beyond that horizon, the line of sight would rise above the surface of the earth so nothing on the surface of the earth beyond the horizon would be visible from the plane. The point is that implications about a horizon not being present if the earth is flat cannot be derived without making additional assumptions, such as that light travels in straight lines. That is, to deduce the consequence that a line of sight would reach to the end of

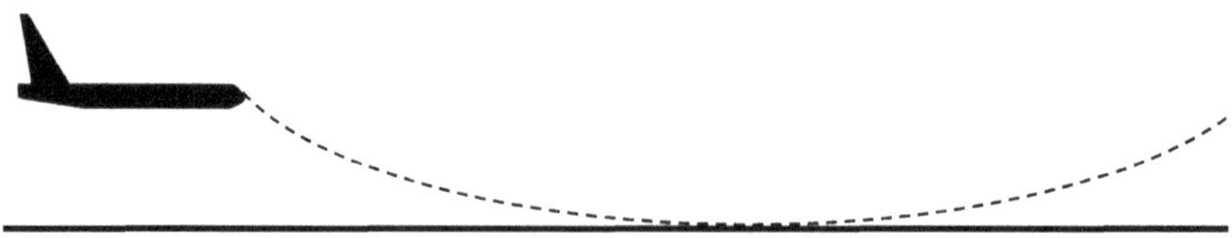

Figure 7.3 If the earth were flat but light rays curved, there would be a horizon beyond which observers could not see the earth's surface

the earth, if the earth were flat, requires the assumption that light travels in straight lines. This is an auxiliary assumption. If that assumption were wrong, the disproof the earth is flat would be wrong. And the assumption that light travels in straight lines could be wrong. Hence, the modus tollens argument using observations from an airplane cannot disprove the earth is flat after all.

Or consider the potential disproof of Newton's laws of gravity because they were apparently violated by the orbit of Uranus. As was noted in Chapter 5, to conclude that the orbit of Uranus violated Newton's laws, a researcher would have to assume there were no nearby planets that could influence Uranus' orbit. Yet this assumption was incorrect. So the incongruous orbit of Uranus did not in fact disprove Newton's laws.

Ladyman (2002) provides another example of a potential falsification of Newtonian mechanics, in this case based on the predicted trajectory of a comet. To derive a comet's future position using Newton's laws of gravity, a researcher would need to know the trajectory and mass of the comet as well as the trajectories and masses of nearby planets. Following the necessary calculations using the required information and Newton's laws of gravity, a researcher could predict the path of the comet and then observe to see if the comet traveled as specified. Any deviation from specification would mean, according to modus tollens, that Newton's laws of gravity were wrong. But a deviation could alternatively be due to a misattribution of any of the trajectories or masses entered into the calculations. Any deviation of the comet from its specified trajectory could thus be explained away, without having to discard Newton's laws. "Clearly, the falsification of a theory by an observation is not as straightforward as the above schema suggests" (Ladyman, 2002, p. 78).

The point is that, although modus tollens is a logically valid argument, it is not an argument that can be applied in practice to disprove hypotheses about nature. The logic applied in practice is based on the following argument:

i If hypothesis H and auxiliary assumptions A are both true, then consequence C must be true.
ii We observe nature and find that consequence C is not true.
iii Therefore, hypothesis H and auxiliary assumptions A are not both true.

The above argument has the following abstract logical form:

i If H and A are both true, then C.
ii C is not true.
iii Therefore, H and A are not both true.

This again is a valid deductive argument—another example of modus tollens or denying the consequent. But it does not prove that hypothesis H is false. It proves only that hypothesis H and assumption A are not both true, which is quite different than proving the hypothesis H is not true. For example, that H and A are not both true could arise when H is true but A is false. To repeat: To derive an empirical consequence of a hypothesis (i.e., to deduce that consequence C would follow from hypothesis H), more than just hypothesis H must be assumed. Auxiliary assumptions A are also required. Then if consequence C is found not to hold, it might be the auxiliary assumptions A that are wrong rather than hypothesis H. That is, when an observation fails to agree with a hypothesis, it may be because the hypothesis is wrong or it may be because an assumption required to deduce that observation (such as that light travels in straight lines) is wrong. As a result, we cannot disprove a hypothesis based on the deductive argument of denying the consequent.

The Duhem-Quine Thesis

That the logical argument of denying the consequent cannot disprove a hypothesis is an implication of the Duhem-Quine thesis, which is also called the principle of holism (Duhem, 1906; Quine, 1951). In words, the Duhem-Quine thesis states that hypotheses are always tested in bundles, never in isolation. By this it is meant that auxiliary assumptions are hypotheses and that the hypothesis of interest cannot be tested without making auxiliary assumptions. You can only evaluate the truth of a claim within a whole network of beliefs. As Duhem (1906/1962) explained in the context of the natural sciences: "An experiment in physics can never condemn an isolated hypothesis but only a whole theoretical group" (p. 183). Yet another way to express the Duhem-Quine thesis is that there will always be alternative explanations for any observations, which was also a conclusion reached in Chapter 6.

An important implication of the Duhem-Quine thesis is that, in the face of apparently disconfirming evidence, a hypothesis can always be saved by altering auxiliary assumptions rather than by abandoning the hypothesis under investigation. That is, if observations appear to refute a hypothesis, a researcher can maintain the hypothesis by altering the auxiliary assumptions. For example, if the earth appears not to be flat, alter the implicit assumption that light travels in straight lines, and observations will now be seen to agree with the hypothesis of a flat earth. Quine (1961) expressed this view: "Any statement can be held true come what may, if we make drastic enough adjustments elsewhere in the system" (p. 43). "*Any* seemingly disconfirming observational evidence can *always* be accommodated to *any* theory" (Klee, 1997, p. 65, emphasis in original).

Interpretations of Data Are Constructed

In the preceding sections, I argued that a hypothesis could not be definitively disproven using an argument in the form of denying the consequent because of a flaw in step i. Step i entails deriving consequences of hypotheses, which requires auxiliary assumptions and those auxiliary assumptions might be wrong. An alternative, but equivalent, way to demonstrate the potential fallibility of denying the consequent is to see that step ii could be in error. Step ii involves observing nature to see if a predicted implication holds true. Step ii can lead to error because observations are subject to error. That is, the observations required to conclude that consequence C is false, as required in step ii of denying the consequent, can be subject to error. That step ii is subject to error is another way of demonstrating that definitive disproof of a hypothesis is impossible. In the previous example of a test of Newton's laws of gravity based on the path of a comet, a discrepancy between data and theory might be due to an error in our empirical observations of the path of the comet. A researcher might have properly deduced where the comet was supposed to be based on Newton's laws (that is, the researcher might have correctly performed step i), but the observation of the comet's position (step ii) might be incorrect.

> When observation and experiment provide evidence that conflicts with the predictions of some law or theory, it may be the evidence that is at fault rather than the law or theory. ... Consequently, straightforward conclusive falsifications of theories by observation are not achievable.
>
> (Chalmers, 2013, pp. 81–82)

As noted in Chapter 1, naïve realism is the belief that we perceive nature as it is—the world is exactly as we see it to be. Naïve realism (also called direct realism and immaculate perception) is the belief that data speak for themselves. Francis Bacon had a related view. According to Bacon, people would be able to definitively see what was true if they could just free their minds from needless bias, which he called Idols (Campbell, 1988b). The truth would be imprinted on the mind if only the mind were empty and passive rather than being susceptible to Idols.

But, as also noted in Chapter 1, naïve realism (as well as Bacon's view) is incorrect. Data do not speak for themselves—they must always be interpreted and we can never be free from Idols. Even our most basic perceptions are constructed by us rather than automatically received. We have no direct access to nature. Our image of the world is not automatically given to us by the world, but constructed by us based on input from the world. When we open our eyes what we see is our construction of nature in our mind rather than nature directly. When we construct a view of nature, we go beyond the data given. That is what construction means. Interpreting (even acquiring a simple sense perception) is an active, constructive process. And because we construct, we can construct incorrectly; we can make mistakes. Think of visual illusions. If we automatically see the world as it is, there could be no visual illusions. Or think of how we see objects in the distance. A large object viewed in the distance can cast only a small image on our retina. But we still *see* the object as large.

Okay, perhaps our vision is constructive and interpretive, but are there not some other means of direct access (perhaps mechanical or technological) that provide knowledge of nature without us having to construct an interpretation? Even if our vision does not give us perfect, infallible access to nature, do not some other methods give us infallible access to nature? No. Data never speak for themselves no matter what form they take. We always have to interpret observations of nature and our interpretations can be wrong. Just as we must construct and make sense of our perceptions, we must also interpret and make sense of the results of any methods used to access reality. No method provides interpretations for us and therefore no method can be assured of giving us a correct interpretation automatically. Even *facts* do not exist independently of people. Nature exists separately from people, but not facts. Facts are statements about nature, and as statements, they are created by people, not nature. There are no facts independent of the knower or independent of assumptions. We construct facts and our constructions can be incorrect.

> There is no nonpresumptive knowledge. All knowledge claims go beyond their evidence, are highly presumptive and corrigible.
>
> (Campbell, 1988a, p. 338)

If even our most basic perceptions and facts are constructed, clearly our more elaborate interpretations of the world are also constructed. The world does not come with interpretations and explanations pre-made. We have to provide interpretations and explanations if we are to understand the world. No matter how obvious and clear-cut an interpretation may appear, it is never provided by the data themselves. Meaning is always attributed to observations, and therefore can be attributed incorrectly.

The Theory-Ladenness of Observation

One reason why even basic perceptions are subject to error is because perceptions are laden with theory, which means beliefs and assumptions influence even basic perception. The theory-ladenness of observation (or the theory-ladenness of facts or the theory-ladenness of experience) is a slogan used to denote the idea that people impose potentially fallible presumptions even when interpreting the most basic of perceptions. There are no perceptions (no matter how basic) that are independent of our presumptions: "there is no such thing as a definite piece of indisputable knowledge about the world whose meaning is not in some way colored by preexisting belief about the world" (Bauer, 1992, p. 65). Hanson (1958) is usually credited with this insight though others had the same insight before Hanson (Phillips, 1987a).

Figures 7.4 and 7.5 provide an example. (Also see Campbell, 1988b, 1988e, and Hanson, 1958, for examples.) The image in Figure 7.4 could be a representation of a pizza or a wheel with spokes. To most observers, Figure 7.4 appears two dimensional. That is, the circle and the straight lines in Figure 7.4 appear to lie in the same plane. In contrast, the lines in Figure 7.5 appear to lie in three dimensions. The reason for the three dimensions is that we impose the presumption that the lines in Figure 7.5 are part of a larger, three-dimensional

Figure 7.4 The image appears to be two-dimensional

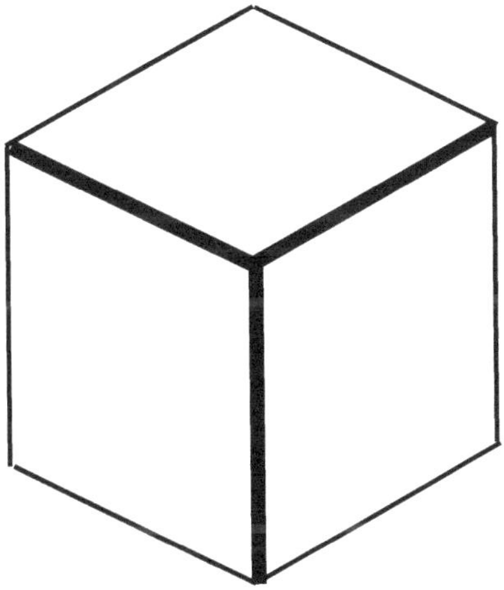

Figure 7.5 The image appears to be three-dimensional but contains three of the same lines in Figure 7.4, which appears to be two-dimensional

object and that presumption influences our perception. In particular, the three darkened lines in Figure 7.5 appear to lie in three dimensions. Yet the three darkened lines in Figure 7.5 also appear as part of Figure 7.4, though they no longer appear to be three dimensional. In the two different contexts, the three identical lines in the two figures appear to be either two dimensional or three dimensional. Perceptions of depth change depending on the presumptions about the two figures. That's the theory-ladenness of observation.

An implication of the theory-ladenness of observation leads to much the same conclusions as have been reached before. The theories with which observations are laden can be incorrect and hence our interpretation of our perceptions can be incorrect. Because the interpretation of observations depends on presumptions, a hypothesis that disagrees with observations cannot be conclusively rejected. Because of errors in the background presumptions, the basic observations might be wrong rather than the hypothesis under investigation. "Thus, observation cannot be a 'neutral foundation', nor a 'disinterested arbiter' of disputes, for the process of observation is influenced (unconsciously) by the theories or hypotheses that the observer holds *before* the observations are made" (Phillips, 1987a, p. 9, emphasis in original).

Disproving is the Complement of Proving

Another argument can be forwarded for why it is impossible to refute a hypothesis decisively. If it were possible to refute a hypothesis decisively, a researcher would be decisively confirming the negation of the hypothesis which is itself a hypothesis. In other words, disconfirming a hypothesis entails confirming the opposite hypothesis: "finding that a statement is false is the same as finding that its negative is true" (Popper, 1972, p. 13). But I have argued in Chapter 6 that it is not possible to decisively confirm a hypothesis. So it must not be possible to decisively disconfirm a hypothesis.

Rejecting Hypotheses versus Rejecting Auxiliary Assumptions

Researchers often do not recognize the truth of the Duhem-Quine thesis because they often do not recognize the auxiliary assumptions being made when observations are interpreted as either supporting or opposing a hypothesis. Nonetheless, scientific practice accedes to the Duhem-Quine thesis because researchers do not willy-nilly reject hypotheses when consequences appear to be disconfirmed. Before a well-accepted hypothesis is rejected based on apparently disconfirming evidence, common practice is to ask first if auxiliary assumptions might be to blame.

> a conflict between a highly confirmed theory and an occasional recalcitrant experiential sentence may well be resolved by revoking the latter rather than by sacrificing the former. Science offers various examples of such procedure.
> (Hempel, 1952, pp. 621–622)

Retaining Newtonian mechanics in the face of the recalcitrant orbit of Uranus is one of the various examples of which Hempel speaks. As will be explained in Chapter 8, the best that can be done in obtaining knowledge of nature is to judge a theory plausible or implausible in the face of both relevant evidence and the plausibility or implausibility of beliefs about auxiliary assumptions. In the face of apparently disconfirming evidence, the researcher assesses whether it is more plausible to reject the hypothesis or the auxiliary assumptions. With the immense wealth of data that supported Newtonian mechanics it was far more plausible to retain Newton's laws of gravity than to reject them in the face of Uranus' apparently anomalous path. But the researcher might always be wrong in assessments of relative plausibility. No evidence can unequivocally lead to the rejection of a hypothesis rather than auxiliary assumptions.

Summary

No disconfirming evidence can logically force a researcher to reject a hypothesis. So there is no way to decisively disconfirm a hypothesis. The logically valid argument of denying the consequent or modus tollens does not provide the means to disprove a hypothesis. Such an apparently definitive argument requires that implications of a hypothesis be derived that can then be assessed with observations. But auxiliary assumptions are always required to derive the implications of a hypothesis. And when observations disagree with implications, it might be the auxiliary assumptions that are wrong rather than the hypothesis to be tested. As the Duhem-Quine thesis specifies, hypotheses are never tested in isolation from auxiliary assumptions, which are never certain. An alternative way to explain the failure of the argument of denying the consequent to disprove a hypothesis is that empirical observations of even correctly derived implications can be mistaken. The theory-ladenness of observations means empirical observations are never free from prior assumptions, which could be wrong.

Combining the lessons from the present chapter with the lessons from the previous chapter, the conclusion is that hypotheses cannot be decisively proven to be either correct or incorrect. "So, sadly, a scientific hypothesis or theory can neither be disproven, nor proven, by means of tests" (Phillips, 1987a, p. 15).

Chapter 8

Abandoning Proof for Plausibility

Chapter 6 demonstrated that researchers cannot decisively prove that a hypothesis about nature is correct. Chapter 7 demonstrated that researchers cannot decisively prove a hypothesis about nature is incorrect. "Thus, *we cannot prove theories and we cannot disprove them either*" (Lakatos, 1978, p. 16, emphasis in original). As a consequence, researchers have to give up any hope that proof can be used as the criterion for justifying their beliefs about nature. Campbell (1988b) makes the same point by referencing our ancestral origins:

> Even if a belief is correct, we cannot know this for certain. … we are cousins to the amoeba, and have received no direct revelations not shared with it. How then, indeed, could we know for certain?
>
> (p. 442)

But if scientists cannot prove that a given hypothesis is either true or false, how do they decide which hypotheses to accept and which not to accept? What is the basis on which scientists should choose among alternative hypotheses? How do scientists determine which beliefs are better warranted than others?

Plausibility Is the Criterion for Belief, Not Proof

The criterion to use in choosing what to believe about nature is not proof or disproof, but plausibility. We can do no better than to believe what is most plausible, not what we can prove or disprove to be true. In choosing among hypotheses, we rest our judgments on the plausibility of the hypotheses.

> In one sense the *best* explanation is the true one. But, having no independent access to which explanatory hypothesis is true, the reasoner can only assert judgments of *best* based on considerations such as plausibility and explanatory power.
>
> (Josephson & Josephson, 1994, p. 15, emphasis in original)

DOI: 10.4324/9781003198413-8

Because researchers cannot rely on proof, they have no choice but to rely on judgments of plausibility. "Plausibility considerations are pervasive in the sciences; they play a significant—indeed, *indispensable*—role" (Salmon, 1998, p. 559, emphasis in original). Basing judgments on plausibility means judgments can be wrong. What is most plausible may not be what is true. Basing judgment on plausibility makes science fallible.

But that science is fallible does not mean it is baseless or that knowledge is unobtainable. The criterion of plausibility might not be as desirable as the criteria of proof and disproof, were those criteria available. But the criterion of plausibility is all we have and it is good enough to warrant some beliefs over others. Popper (1968) made it clear that "*We do not know: we can only guess*" (p. 278, emphasis in original). But some guesses are better than others:

> just because there exist alternative theoretical explanations for a given collection of observational data doesn't mean that all those alternative explanations are equally plausible and equally likely to be correct .... *Not all theoretical alternatives are equal.*
>
> (Klee, 1997, p. 177, emphasis in original)

Showing a hypothesis is plausible while other hypotheses are implausible is an advance in knowledge. "...knowledge is possible even in the face of uncertainty" (Josephson & Josephson, 1994, p. 16). The point can be made even more forcefully. Hempel (1966) explained how knowledge is possible in the face of uncertainty thusly:

> But the observation that a favorable outcome of however many tests does not afford conclusive proof for a hypothesis should not lead us to think that if we have subjected a hypothesis to a number of tests and all of them have had a favorable outcome, we are no better off than if we had not tested the hypothesis at all.
>
> (p. 8)

And Phillips (1992c, 1992a) explained why not all claims to knowledge are equally justified:

> although no knowledge is certain, not all knowledge-claims are equal; some are better warranted than others in the sense that they have survived serious critique and strenuous attempts at overthrow. ... if any inquiry that is careless about evidence is as acceptable as an inquiry that has taken pains to be precise and unbiased, then there is no need to inquire—we might as well accept, without further fuss, any old view that tickles our fancy.
>
> (pp. 15 and 61)

Importantly, the multiple hypotheses method is well suited to using plausibility as the criterion for belief. As noted in Chapter 3, the MH method specifies that a person is justified in tentatively accepting hypothesis X, if the evidence is in good agreement with hypothesis X and not nearly in as good agreement with any of the alternatives to hypothesis X. That the evidence is in good agreement with hypothesis X means hypothesis X is plausible, given the evidence. That the evidence is not nearly in as good agreement with any of the alternatives to hypothesis X means hypothesis X is more plausible than any of the alternatives, given the evidence. In other words, according to the MH method, a researcher accepts a hypothesis both if it is plausible given the available evidence and if it is more plausible than any of the alternative hypotheses given the available evidence. And note that the alternative hypotheses that can be considered include the failure of auxiliary assumptions (see Chapter 7). The MH method does not prove that hypothesis X is correct. All this process does is provide good reasons for making decisions and taking actions based on hypothesis X.

Even though we can neither prove nor disprove a hypothesis about nature, choosing to believe the hypothesis that is most plausible after comparison with diligently identified alternative hypotheses based on diligently obtained data, is a rational course of action. The MH method applied using the criterion of plausibility provides a rational justification for beliefs. And we are justified in taking actions and making decisions based on the beliefs of what is most plausible using the MH method.

A Bayesian View

Sometimes it will be difficult to decide which hypothesis among many is most plausible. In addition, different people can legitimately disagree about what hypothesis is most plausible because they have different background knowledge and hold different pre-existing assumptions. Plausibility is a very personal decision based on a researcher's own beliefs and proclivities. As a result, what is judged most plausible is subjective. "So an element of subjective judgement, or scientific common sense, will often be needed to decide among competing theories" (Okasha, 2016, p. 85). That judgments are based on what is subjectively most plausible rather than what can be proven true makes science a very human endeavor, rather than a mechanical one.

But while judgments of what is most plausible is subjective, as more and more observations are obtained the plausibility of some hypotheses is likely to increase while that of others is likely to decrease and there will often be a consensus across people. Adding evidence that diverges from a person's beliefs should tend to change that person's beliefs. As shown in Chapter 6, it is not possible to prove tooth fairies do not exist or that desks do. There are always alternative explanations for all the available data. But given the evidence generally available, most people would agree it is highly plausible that tooth fairies do not exist and that desks do.

That adding evidence should tend to change beliefs is a Bayesian outcome. There appears to be disagreement about whether a person has a choice of being a Bayesian. But there should be relatively little disagreement. If you accept the premises of probability theory and can abide by a subjectivist interpretation of probability, you are a Bayesian (Brand, 1976, 1979). The premises of probability theory are highly plausible. Those premises include such things as the following: (1) probabilities are between zero and one, (2) an event that will certainly occur has probability equal to one, (3) an event that will certainly not occur has probability equal to zero, and (4) the probability of A and B, where these are two mutually exclusive events, is equal to the probability of A plus the probability of B. It is difficult not to accept these premises of probability. Similarly, a subjectivist interpretation of probability is widespread. If you can assign a probability to one-of-a-kind future events, you are a subjectivist at heart. For example, if you can assign a probability that your favorite sports team will have a winning record next year, you are likely assigning probability according to subjectivist tenets. If you accept the premises of probability theory and assign probabilities subjectively, Bayes theorem necessarily follows, which makes you a Bayesian. This does not mean you must use Bayesian statistical methods. But it does mean, to be consistent in your beliefs, you must change your beliefs in the face of good evidence.

Researchers should never be certain in their beliefs about nature. That is one thing learned from the preceding chapters. Researchers can be highly convinced but never completely certain. But according to Bayesian probability, researchers' beliefs should be altered (even if only slightly) by newly acquired and credible evidence. And with enough additional evidence, researchers' beliefs should be changed to be in agreement with the new evidence, and to deviate from prior beliefs, to the extent the evidence deviates from our prior beliefs. This tends to be the way science works. Not all scientists change their beliefs. But as the data pile up in contradiction to cherished beliefs, the scientific consensus tends to follow suit. Phillips (1987b) provides an example from the natural sciences:

> just because a scientist holds the view—supported by his or her theory—that magnetic monopoles exist, it does not follow that he or she will detect such contentious objects. And if some are detected, almost certainly those scientists who previously did not believe in monopoles will be won over.
>
> (p. 87)

Sagan (1991) also argues that scientists change their minds:

> It doesn't happen as often as it should, because scientists are human and change is sometimes painful. But it happens every day.
>
> (p. 5).

Changing one's belief is partly what separates scientists from pseudoscientists (also see Chapter 5). To the extent scientists gratuitously do not change their views in the face of overwhelming evidence to the contrary of their beliefs, they are acting as pseudoscientists. As shown in Chapter 7, it can be appropriate to maintain belief in a hypothesis in the face of apparently disconfirming evidence. But ultimately data must be the arbiter of our beliefs if scientists are to practice good science. Ultimately, beliefs must be brought into agreement with ever accumulating empirical evidence, if researchers are to be scientific—if researchers are to make strong inferences. This is not the way pseudoscience works. Even as evidence piles up, beliefs within the pseudoscientific community do not change. To not change beliefs in the face of discordant and persistent data is to act as a pseudoscientist.

Disconfirming evidence is evidence that suggests a hypothesis is incorrect. Confirming evidence is evidence that suggests a hypothesis is correct. In many places, Popper (1965, 1968) argues that disconfirming evidence is more valuable than confirming evidence. Others disagree (Chalmers, 2013; Lakatos, 1970). From a Bayesian perspective, confirming evidence is as valuable as disconfirming evidence. Evidence of all sorts changes a person's beliefs within a Bayesian framework.

More on the Underdetermination of Theory by Observation

Chapter 6 argued that theories (or hypotheses) were underdetermined by observation. This meant there was always more than one hypothesis that could explain all the available evidence. Indeed, it is possible for the available evidence to be explained by an infinite number of hypotheses. Hence it was impossible to prove that any one hypothesis is correct because no available evidence uniquely determines that hypothesis.

As also noted in Chapter 6, that there are always alternative hypotheses that can explain any set of data is called the problem of the underdetermination of theory by observation. It might be argued that the underdetermination of theory by observation makes science impossible. The argument is that if data cannot be used to choose among hypotheses decisively because of underdetermination, then there is no way at all to choose among hypotheses. This view is called radical underdetermination. But this view fails. It is true that the underdetermination of theory by observation means data cannot be used to choose among hypotheses decisively. But, as I have just argued above, data can often be used to choose among hypotheses based on judgments of what is most plausible. In other words, data can make some hypotheses more plausible than others. And that is how researchers can chooses among hypotheses. Not just any alternative hypothesis is plausible simply because it could, in principle, account for all the available evidence. Logical possibility is not enough to believe a hypothesis. To believe a hypothesis is true, it must be plausible in the face of the available evidence. And all hypotheses that could account for the available evidence are not all equally plausible.

The younger brother in Chapter 6 can argue that the hypothesis that tooth fairies exist is compatible with any and all data that are available. But that hypothesis is not nearly as plausible (given the wealth of data available) as the hypothesis that tooth fairies do not exist. Similarly, I can argue the data do not logically contradict the hypothesis there is no desk in front of me. But I cannot plausibly maintain that hypothesis. In spite of the underdetermination of theory by observation, science is possible because science operates based on the criterion of plausibility rather than proof. "[Our] cognitive equipment has been selected for discovering significant truths about the environment. Indeed, natural selection has conferred such powers on human cognition that we need not take the underdetermination of science by evidence very seriously" (Rosenberg, 2012, p. 247).

More on the Duhem-Quine Thesis

Chapter 7 introduced the Duhem-Quine thesis, which is the thesis that no hypothesis is ever tested in isolation. Deriving observable implications of a hypothesis always requires making auxiliary assumptions and it is the combination of hypothesis and auxiliary assumptions that is being tested when assessing observable implications, rather than the hypothesis alone. As a result, even if observable implications do not hold true, it is not possible to decisively conclude the hypothesis is false. That is, the Duhem-Quine thesis provides another explanation for why there is no way to disprove a hypothesis decisively. An investigator can always blame the auxiliary assumptions for any failure to find predicted observable implications and thereby retain the hypothesis under investigation.

However, even though the Duhem-Quine thesis means no hypothesis can be decisively disproved, there are other ways to rule out hypotheses. The other ways to rule out hypotheses are based on the criterion of plausibility, rather than proof. If the auxiliary assumptions are well supported by other evidence (i.e., if the auxiliary assumptions are highly plausible), it might be highly implausible to maintain the favored hypothesis in the face of disconfirming data. Auxiliary assumptions can often be tested in ways independent of the hypothesis under investigation. And these tests might provide evidence that makes the auxiliary assumptions highly plausible. In which case, it can be more plausible to reject the hypothesis under investigation than to reject the auxiliary assumptions. The Quine-Duhem hypothesis provides researchers a ready excuse for maintaining belief in a hypothesis in spite of conflicting evidence. Even statements about nature that are wildly inconsistent with sense data can be maintained. "This does not, however, mean that one may *justifiably* or *rationally* believe a statement regardless of the experience that one had had" (Staley, 2014, p. 35, emphasis in original).

A researcher can always adjust assumptions or find some ad hoc assumptions to impose so as to salvage a favored hypothesis from apparently disconfirming evidence. But those ad hoc assumptions had better have independent empirical support. If the implications of the ad hoc assumptions are not confirmed by data, the research program will be degenerative rather than progressive (Lakatos, 1970). If favored hypotheses were always being salvaged by adding ad hoc assumptions, hypotheses would proliferate without any hypotheses being winnowed out. But hypotheses do get discarded in scientific practice. Science is able to operate in spite of the Duhem-Quine thesis because its criterion for rejection of hypotheses is what is most plausible, not what can be disproven. Not all hypotheses are equally plausible, given the empirical evidence. And the relatively implausible hypotheses can be and are often discarded (at least tentatively).

> The Quine-Duhem equivocality of any experimental result is a very real problem .... It can only be resolved by discretionary judgments of plausibility. Nonetheless, scientific communities often achieve working consensus, often against the interests of the established and powerful.
>
> (Campbell, 1988f, p. 519)

But I should be quick to note that, in practice, discarding a favored hypothesis requires more than discordant data. As Hempel (1966) and Lakatos (1968, 1970, 1978) emphasized, a hypothesis is not to be dismissed because of discordant data unless, in addition, an alternative hypothesis is available that plausibly explains the data the original hypothesis did and provides new, corroborated implications. In practice, the presence of falsifying observations is not sufficient by itself to reject a hypothesis:

> *no experiment, experimental report, observational statement or well-corroborated low-level falsifying hypothesis alone can lead to falsification. There is no falsification before the emergence of a better theory.*
>
> (Lakatos, 1978, p. 35, emphasis in original)

More on the Theory-Ladenness of Observation

Chapter 7 described the theory-ladenness of observation, which states that our prior beliefs influence even our most basic perceptions. Accordingly, when testing a hypothesis using empirical observations (as required by either the H-D or the MH method), scientists inevitably impose assumptions based on their prior beliefs. As a result, it is sometimes argued, hypotheses cannot be tested in an unbiased fashion, which renders fair-minded science impossible. "If there is no theory-neutral observation, then the empirical world can no longer serve as an objective arbiter among competing hypotheses" (Gorham, 2009, p. 83), which some people argue neuters science. That is, if a scientist presumes a theory in making a set of observations, the observations will necessarily conform to the theory so it would be impossible to reject the theory with the observations. Thankfully, this argument is not persuasive. While it is true that observations are always laden with theory, the theory with which the observations are laden need not be the same as the theory or hypothesis under test. To the extent the hypothesis under test is not being imposed as an a priori belief when making the observations, a test of the hypothesis can be performed free from bias due to the theory-ladenness of observation. And in general, the theories with which the observations are laden are not the same as the theories under test. So tests unbiased by the theory-ladenness of observations can be conducted.

For example, scientists do, on many occasions, decide their hypotheses are wrong in the presence of recalcitrant evidence. Such decisions of wrongness could not occur if observations were always laden with the hypothesis being tested. And scientists who hold widely different hypotheses about nature will nonetheless often agree about the interpretation of basic data. Tycho Brahe collected extensive data on the relative positions of celestial objects based on his presupposition that the sun revolved around the earth. But rather than being imbued with that presupposition, Kepler used those very observations to support the opposite conclusion: that the earth revolved around the sun (Campbell, 1988b; Phillips, 1992a). Or consider another example. We are certainly predisposed to presume a Euclidean interpretation of reality yet such presumptions do not stop us from accepting the non-Euclidean interpretation of nature in Einstein's general theory of relativity (Godfrey-Smith, 2003). Our eyes cannot always trick us into seeing whatever we want or expect. As Chalmers (2013) explains:

> Another point that serves to get the "theory-dependence of experiment" in perspective is that, however informed by theory an experiment is, there is a strong sense in which the results of an experiment are determined by the world and not by the theories. … We cannot make the outside world conform to our theories. … It is the sense in which experimental outcomes are determined by the workings of the world rather than by theoretical views about the world that provides the possibility of testing theories against the world.
>
> (p. 36)

The point of raising the concept of the theory-ladenness of observation in Chapter 7 was to provide another reason why data cannot lead to a decisive disproof of a hypothesis. The theory-ladenness of observation implies that the interpretation of observation is fallible. Hence it might be the interpretation of an observation rather than a hypothesis that might be at fault when an observation appears to deviate from the prediction derived from a hypothesis. As a result, the deviant observation does not decisively disprove the hypothesis. But, again, the notion of plausibility is relevant. Rather than disproving a hypothesis decisively, the best that can be done is to show that a hypothesis is implausible. To do so, a researcher need not interpret observations decisively but need do no more than interpret observations plausibly. That is, interpretations of observations need not be definitively correct, merely plausible. If it is more plausible to trust the interpretation of an observation than to retain a hypothesis in the face of an apparently deviant observation, it can be reasonably concluded that the hypothesis is not in good agreement with the data. Such a conclusion is all that is required to implement the MH method. The theory-ladenness of observation need not restrict our ability to judge what is most plausible.

Abandoning Infallibility

We have now seen that researchers cannot definitively prove or disprove a hypothesis about nature. Researchers must proceed using the criterion of plausibility rather than proof. The point is that researchers can never know the state of nature with certainty. But might researchers be able to argue plausibly that their views are nonetheless always correct, even though they cannot be proven to be correct? Even though researchers can never be certain, might it still be reasonable to believe that their views are nonetheless infallible? Is it reasonable to believe scientists never make mistakes? Might the criterion of plausibility be sufficient to get to the truth about reality without error? The answer is clearly no. An argument for infallibility is unsustainable in the face of the plausible interpretations of overwhelming evidence of scientists' many apparent mistakes. We have to abandon decisive proof and disproof. And researchers have to abandon the notion, if they ever held it, that their beliefs are infallible.

Visual illusions are examples of errors people make in even the most basic perceptions. And even if basic perceptions were always correct there is no assurance that the more elaborate and cherished hypotheses about nature are always correct. That scientists have often believed contradictory hypotheses demonstrates that at least some scientists are wrong at least some of the time. If scientists believe hypothesis X and later disbelieve hypothesis X, it is not possible that both beliefs are correct. Scientists believed in Newtonian laws of motion for two hundred years while currently those beliefs are superseded by Einstein's theory of relativity. And some now believe that relativity theory is incorrect, or at least limited, though the replacement theory is not yet clear. The theory of continental drift was rejected for years even though it is now widely accepted as true. Scientists used to believe in phlogiston (which was a purported substance in combustible material that was released causing combustion) but they do not any longer. Scientists used to believe there was an ether that pervaded space but now believe an ether was illusory. Scientists used to believe in the caloric theory of heat. But scientists now believe in the kinetic theory of heat (Goldstein & Goldstein, 1984). The theory of evolution by natural selection was once controversial and still is among some people, while the majority of scientists swear by it (Dobzhansky, 1973). Scientists also sometimes fail in deriving appropriate consequences of hypotheses for observation. Tycho Brahe thought data convincingly disconfirmed the idea the earth moved because he could not find the presumably required parallax in the position of the stars. It turned out the stars were much further away than Brahe had assumed so his disconfirmation was flawed (Brown, 1977; Chalmers, 2013). Or at least that is what scientists believe now. The point is scientists can be and have often been wrong. Almost certainly scientists have and will continue to make many mistakes in their beliefs about nature. Scientists can't even be certain they are making progress toward understanding nature in their research:

> It is now recognized more clearly than ever before that our human judgments about what *is* true are fallible, and subject to constant revision. And it is recognized that we cannot even be sure that our constant revisions are bringing us nearer to the truth.
>
> (Phillips, 1992b, pp. 108–109, emphasis in original)

But I might quickly add that it is plausible that we are getting nearer to the truth, though not always in a straight line trajectory.

There is another reason to believe scientific knowledge can be wrong. That is because science is conducted by humans and humans suffer from cognitive biases. Confirmation bias is a prominent example of a cognitive bias. Confirmation bias means humans (both scientists and nonscientists) are swayed more by evidence that conforms to their prior beliefs than by evidence that opposes their prior beliefs. People are swayed more by confirming than disconfirming evidence in a number of ways. People seek out confirming evidence more than they seek out opposing evidence. This leads people to be swayed by confirming evidence more than opposing evidence because confirming evidence becomes more prevalent. People also evaluate evidence differently depending upon whether it confirms rather than disconfirms their prior beliefs. Evidence that confirms prior beliefs tends to be accepted at face value. Evidence that challenges prior beliefs tends to be subjected to further scrutiny to find uncertainties in the evidence, which are always present. People also interpret ambiguous evidence in ways that support prior beliefs rather than challenge them. People remember evidence that supports their prior beliefs better than people remember information that contradicts their prior beliefs. And so on. Because of such effects, people's prior beliefs are harder to overthrow than they should be. This means people can remain susceptible to error more than they should. People's beliefs have an inertia that is not appropriately justified by evidence.

Humans suffer from innumerable other cognitive biases as well. For example, Tversky and Kahneman (1982) have documented a wide range of heuristics that people use in judging the likelihood of events. For example, people judge events that come to mind more easily (i.e., are more vivid in memory) to be more likely than events that do not come to mind as easily. This vividness effect is based on what is called the availability heuristic. Heuristics help people make decisions quickly and simplify the complex tasks of making judgments about the probabilities of uncertain events. And heuristics generally lead to correct decisions. It's just that the heuristics do not always work well. For example, what is most vivid in memory is not always what is most likely. Heuristics provide predictable methods for making judgments but, in doing so, also tend to produce predictable errors.

For another example, people tend to be over confident in their beliefs. Once people come up with an explanation for a phenomenon, they are often more convinced it is correct than they should be. And people become emotionally attached to their beliefs (Chamberlin, 1890/1965). People are less willing to admit their beliefs are potentially in error than they should be.

My listings of scientific mistakes and cognitive biases are not meant to suggest that humans are generally poor at evaluating evidence and revising their beliefs. Just the opposite tends to be true. People's abilities to sense the world and interpret evidence are quite sophisticated, having been developed through natural evolution so people can successfully interact with the world (as explained in more detail in Chapter 9). The point is simply that people are fallible and do, in fact, make mistakes.

The good news is that scientists are well aware of cognitive biases and have studied them so they can be understood and so their influences can be minimized. In addition, scientific methods have evolved so as to correct for many of the errors potentially introduced by cognitive biases. For example, the MH method specifies that researchers diligently identify plausible alternative hypotheses including those that are opposed to prior beliefs. The MH method also specifies that researchers diligently collect evidence even if it opposes prior beliefs, and then revise their beliefs as appropriate. Both specifications make researchers less susceptible to confirmation, and other, biases.

Summary

Researchers must be satisfied with plausibility as the criterion for their beliefs. Researchers cannot prove their beliefs about nature are correct. Nor can researchers disprove their beliefs. At best, researchers can do no better than believe what is most plausible. This means our beliefs must forever remain uncertain and potentially fallible. Indeed, it seems highly plausible that even the most cherished beliefs have often been wrong. The MH method is fully compatible with both plausibility as the criterion for beliefs and with the fallibility of beliefs as the necessary state of affairs. The MH method does not assume proof or infallibility. According to the MH method, researchers should accept those hypotheses that are most plausible in the face of empirical evidence. The MH method is also self-correcting in the face of errors. By constantly and diligently seeking alternative hypotheses and new evidence, the MH method provides the means to continually challenge the hypotheses researchers currently judge most plausible and even resurrect hypotheses previously judged implausible. The MH method provides means of coping with the inability to prove or disprove hypotheses, and the resulting inevitable fallibility.

Chapter 9

Justifying the Multiple Hypotheses Method

The preceding chapter showed that the criterion for beliefs about nature must be plausibility rather than proof or disproof and, as a result, science is fallible. The question must therefore be asked how we can justify the multiple hypotheses method if it does not offer proof of the truth of our hypotheses about nature and thereby does not guarantee infallibility. If the MH method cannot produce proof and is fallible why are we justified in using it?

I think the best justification is that the MH method is the method by which science operates when science is done well. Even though the literature often describes science as if it uses the hypothetico-deductive method, when science is at its best, it ultimately operates according to the multiple hypotheses method. As per the MH method, scientists diligently identify alternative hypotheses and diligently collect evidence to choose among alternative hypotheses. Scientists may focus on a single hypothesis at any one time, using a circumscribed set of data, as per the H-D method. But the overarching structure of science is to put all the plausible alternative hypotheses that can be identified into a survival-of-the-fittest competition using all the evidence that can be mustered. The H-D method is often espoused, but the MH method is ultimately used in science to justify our beliefs about nature. Authors need to correct their writings so the MH method is presented rather than the H-D method. One of the primary purposes of this book is to encourage authors to more accurately describe science in terms of the MH method rather than in terms of the H-D method.

Examples and proponents of the MH method abound. Acknowledging and attending to alternative explanations and rival hypotheses is the accepted norm in many methodological writings and in much of practice. For example, the Campbellian (Shadish, Cook, & Campbell, 2002) approach to causal inference, which is explicitly focused on ruling out rival hypotheses, is widely accepted across the social sciences. The American Psychological Association's (APA, 2020) widely used *Publication Manual* makes clear that alternative hypotheses (which often consist of threats to internal validity) for a researcher's results are to be acknowledged forthrightly:

> Your interpretation of the results should take into account (a) sources of potential bias and other threats to internal validity, (b) the imprecision of measures, (c) the overall number of tests and/or overlap of tests, (d) the

DOI: 10.4324/9781003198413-9

> adequacy of sample sizes and sampling validity, and (e) other limitations or weaknesses of the study.
>
> (p. 90)

I would argue that reporting limitations and weaknesses of the study should include discussing alternative hypotheses for the results that still remain plausible even after efforts to rule them implausible. In agreement with the APA guidelines, Cochran (1965) suggested that all empirical research reports should be required to include a separate section entitled *Validity of the Results*, wherein plausible alternative hypotheses are acknowledged and rebutted to the extent data allow. Although many textbooks on the methods of scientific research present the scientific method as if it is the H-D method, the later chapters in these same textbooks usually insist its readers attend to plausible alternative hypotheses in the form of threats to internal validity and give readers the tools for doing so.

Justifying Science

The preceding claim that the multiple hypotheses method is justified because it is how science operates raises the obvious question of how, in turn, to justify science. Just as researchers cannot prove a hypothesis about nature is true, researchers cannot prove that science is the best way to accumulate knowledge of nature. Scientists cannot even prove that science is an adequate way to accumulate knowledge (Kuhn, 1970). But the success of science is highly plausible. It is plausible that science works well as a means of acquiring knowledge of reality for several reasons.

The Evolution of our Senses. Science is based on empirical evidence, which is evidence generated by our senses (e.g., sight, touch, smell, hearing, and taste). Empirical evidence is the fundamental building block for science. To the extent our senses generally work well, there is reason to trust the foundation upon which science is based.

The reason to trust our senses and our interpretations of basic sense data is that they have both evolved so as to well recognize the world as it is, in the situations in which we most often find ourselves. It is evolutionarily adaptive to have senses, and ways of interpreting our basic sense data, that are accurate. That is, our perceptual apparatus (both sense organs and our brains) have developed following Darwinian evolution to sustain our survival. If basic sense data were typically misinterpreted, humans would likely not have endured as a species.

Citing Lorenz (1941), Campbell (1988c) likens the brain's evolved ability to understand the world to the adaptation of the horse's hoof to the surface of the earth. The horse's hoof has evolved to serve the horse well in its travels. So, too, the human brain has evolved to serve humans well in the cognitive domains in which it exists. The brain makes mistakes, just as the horse can sometimes misstep. But had not human brains adapted over the ages to recognize the world largely as it is, humans would not have well survived based on their intelligence rather than their brute strength, just as horses would not have well survived to live on the plains and navigate effectively.

> The shape of the horse's hoof certainly expresses "knowledge" of the steppe in a very odd and partial language .... Our visual, tactual, and several modes of scientific knowledge ... are comparably objective.
>
> (Campbell, 1988c, p. 430)

Yes, people are susceptible to visual illusions which show that their senses are not always reliable. But scientists are aware of visual illusions. Scientists can take a ruler or other reliable measuring device and determine the truth when they suffer from a visual illusion (Campbell, 1988b). If scientists could not discover they are sometimes wrong and correct their mistakes, they would never be aware that visual illusions exist. In addition, visual illusions are not the norm. Scientists do not typically find, using rulers or other measuring instruments, that visual perceptions and their interpretations are illusory. Scientists have studied basic perception, know much about it, and plausibly know it can be highly accurate in most situations. And scientists know a lot about when perceptions are flawed so they can correct for the effects of perceptual biases. As Godfrey-Smith (2003) argues, scientists well understand the science of perception:

> we have good reason to believe that observation is a generally reliable way of forming beliefs. ... humans are biological organisms embedded in a physical world that we evolved to deal with. ... There is a kind of 'underdetermination' here, as psychologists themselves often say. However, we *can* in fact make reliable judgements about what is around us, using perceptual mechanisms. And we can know that we are able to do this, by studying the operation of our perceptual mechanisms scientifically. In the case of perception, we can learn *what kind of reliability we have* in our attempts to know about the world.
>
> (pp. 65, 222–223, emphasis in original)

Of course, I have not proved that people's senses are generally reliable. All I have argued is that it is highly plausible that people's senses are generally reliable. That is enough to begin to build a plausible justification of science. Yes, no one knows for certain that human perceptions are not all hallucinations and dreams or that human brains are not all in a vat with their perceptions controlled by an all-powerful computer. But that is highly implausible. The reason for the implausibility of hallucinations, dreams, and brain-in-a-vat hypotheses, according to Wimsatt (1981), is the consistency, or robustness, of our sense perceptions:

> Robustness is widely used as a criterion for the reliability or trustworthiness of the thing which is said to be robust. The boundaries of an ordinary object, such as a table, as detected in different sensory modalities (visually,

> tactually, aurally, orally), roughly coincide, making them robust; and this is ultimately the primary reason why we regard perception of the object as veridical rather than illusory .... It is a rare illusion indeed which could systematically affect all of our senses in that consistent manner. (Drug-induced hallucinations and dreams may involve multimodal experience but fail to be consistent through time for a given subject, or across observers, thus failing at a higher level to show appropriate robustness.)
>
> (p. 144)

The same argument could be made about common sense knowing. At bedrock, science is just refined common sense as acknowledged by both Popper (1972, p. 34, emphasis in original) ("*all science, and all philosophy, are enlightened common sense*") and Einstein (2003, p. 23) ("The whole of science is nothing more than a refinement of everyday thinking"). And common sense has evolved over the millennia to have survival value.

Science Is Successful. Science appears to work quite well in providing knowledge of the natural world. Clearly science does not automatically lead to truth. But science has quite plausibly produced wonderful successes such as in technology, public health, medicine, economic development, and understanding nature. Science is responsible for our abilities to construct skyscrapers, create electronic wonders, and explore the universe. "Science does in fact have a magnificent track record of technological application with practical, pragmatic success" (Rosenberg, 2012, p. 249). And science is capable of accurately predicting myriad outcomes including the path of comets, the flight of cannon balls and the regularity of the tides (Gorham, 2009).

How do scientists know these apparent achievements are real rather than illusory? Scientists cannot prove that science has led to the right answers in technology, public health, medicine, economic development, and understanding nature. But it seems exceptionally plausible that science has helped to successfully guide our actions in innumerable ways. That is, there is lots of compelling evidence of the success of science. In addition, science seems to work better than any other method for understanding nature and making advances in the human condition.

> For down the long haul of human time, no other social institution whose job it is or was to keep the epistemological part of the human project going has ever amassed such an impressive record of success—predictive success, explanatory success, and manipulative success [as science].
>
> (Klee, 1997, p. 239)

I've argued scientists cannot know the nature of reality for certain and scientists can't even know for certain that science is progressing more and more accurately toward truth over time. But remember that certainty is not the currency of science. It is highly plausible that scientific knowledge is slowly, though not inexorably and not without backtracking, advancing our understanding of reality: "while we can never have sufficiently good arguments in the empirical sciences for claiming that we have actually reached the truth, we can have strong and reasonably good arguments for claiming that we have made progress towards the truth" (Gorham, 2009, p. 100, attributed to Popper).

Science Is Self-Correcting. The MH method produces only tentative conclusions as the result of a never-ending iterative process of investigation. Alternative hypotheses are diligently identified and investigated. A hypothesis that was tentatively accepted can later be superseded by an alternative hypothesis. Those hypotheses that do not pass muster at one point in time are set to the side but can be resurrected if further data provide adequate support later on. Such changes are not just theoretical possibilities. There are abundant examples where scientists have corrected their views to better align with incoming data. The implementation of the MH method makes science self-correcting. "There have been enough cases of successful theories being amended in unexpected ways, or of unforeseen new phenomena being discovered, for it to be apparent that even the finest science is subject to revision and correction" (Ladyman, 2002, p. 232). No scientific knowledge provides the indubitable foundation upon which to construct certain understanding of the world. But science's ability for self-correction allows it to sustain and overcome error.

Scientists must rely on presumptions which are potentially fallible. But those presumptions can be challenged and corrected. Of course, scientists cannot challenge all their suppositions at once. Scientists impose those presumptions that seem most plausible and then base their thinking on those presumptions as if they are foundational. But scientists can go back later and challenge those presumptions and revise them as needed. Nothing is accepted as certain. Everything is up for revision. Campbell (1988a) likened scientists to sailors at sea who must replace a rotting hull plank by plank. In such an endeavor, scientists must rely

> on the relative soundness of all of the other planks while we replace a particularly weak one. Each of the planks we now depend on we will in turn have to replace. No one of them is a foundation, nor point of certainty, no one of them is incorrigible.
>
> (Campbell, 1988a, p. 338)

The need for, and success of, constant revision and correction is aided and abetted by the social structure of science. Scientists form a disputatious community of scholars who critique each other's hypothesizing (Campbell, 1988f). Dissent and argument among scholars is the hallmark of science. Scientific peers are rightfully skeptical and are the steady source of alternative hypotheses, additional empirical tests of other scientists' most cherished beliefs, and reinterpretations of evidence (Krathwohl, 1985). All scientific thinking is subjected to scrutiny by others, if not by oneself. Skepticism is encouraged in science rather than avoided as in pseudoscience. That even its most foundational presumptions can be challenged means that science can self-correct even its most foundational presumptions.

Scientific Methods Have Evolved. Just as our brains and perceptual apparatuses have evolved, so have scientific methods. Scientists have learned to recognize potential biases in their methods and have devised ever improving techniques to correct for sources of errors. For example, scientists have studied confirmation biases (and other effects of expectations) and have developed techniques, such as masking (aka double blinding procedures), to cope with them. When estimating effects, scientists have devised sophisticated methods for creating control and comparison groups to estimate effects free from threats to internal validity (Reichardt, 2019; Shadish, Cook, & Campbell, 2002). Scientists have learned they cannot trust correlations in data to unambiguously reveal the truth about cause and effect. Scientists have developed statistical methods to rule out chance as an alternative explanation. Scientific thinking and the methods of science have evolved so scientists can avoid misleading themselves, which means they can be more likely to learn the truth. The advance in scientific methods is an empirical accomplishment in that scientists have learned what works and what does not work from self-critical experience.

Begging the Question

The point I have made so far in this chapter is that there are plausible reasons to believe the multiple hypotheses method is a good means (indeed, the best means) for understanding the world. A careful reader will have noticed, however, that my argument is circular. I have justified the MH method by arguing it is the method by which the science best operates. Then I have argued it is plausible to believe that science works well. In so doing, I have not proven the MH method works well but have merely provided plausible reasons to believe the MH method works well, where those reasons themselves are based on what is most plausible. I have built a justification for the MH method to use plausibility as the criterion for what to believe based on accepting what is most plausible to believe about the MH method and science. In simple terms, my argument is that it is plausible to trust plausibility. Plausibility justifies plausibility.

I respond to a criticism of circularity in three ways. First, because there is no way to prove a hypothesis about nature is true, there is no way to prove that any method of learning about the world produces truth. In defending the MH method as a means for understanding the world, the best that can be done is to demonstrate it works better than any alternatives, such as the H-D method and pseudoscience. And in such comparisons, no plausible alternative has been shown to be superior to the MH method as a means to conduct science. In turn, no alternative to science has been shown superior as a means for understanding reality. In understanding the world, the best that can be done is to demonstrate that our knowledge is plausible, in the face of diligently identified alternative hypotheses and diligently obtained evidence. Proof is beyond our reach. It is unreasonable to expect a justification of a method for warranting knowledge using any criterion other than plausibility.

Second, circular reasoning is sometimes the best that can be done in justifying one's thinking. For example, rationality is certainly defensible, is it not? But it is not possible to justify rationality without using a rational argument, which is circular reasoning.

> We are bound to run into trouble if we seek rational justification of every principle we use, for we cannot provide a *rational argument* for rational argument itself without assuming what we are arguing for. Not even logic can be *argued for* in a way that is not question begging.
>
> (Chalmers, 2013, p. 49, emphasis in original)

Just as it is not possible to provide a justification of rationality without being rational it is not possible to produce a sound critique of rationality without using a rational argument. As a result, any sound critique of rationality would suffer from internal inconsistency. Alternatively, it might be possible to mount a defense of rationality on pragmatic grounds. Rational argument is widely accepted by serious thinkers. To challenge rationality would be to challenge the very foundation of human intellectual pursuit. It is not clear what could adequately replace rationality.

The same justifications hold for science as for rationality. In particular, it is not clear what reasonable alternative there is to rigorous science as a means to well understand reality. In addition, assuming rationality is justifiable, rationality can be used in turn to justify science: "There is not even anything irrational in relying for practical purposes upon well-tested theories, for no more rational course of action is open to us" (Popper, 1965, p. 51).

Third, circular reasoning need not be fatal to an argument. Consider the defense of circularity offered by Campbell (1988b):

> Quine and Shimony recognize the circularity of assuming knowledge in the process of justifying knowledge, but provide subtle arguments that such circularity need not be vacuous or vicious.
>
> (p. 444)

And consider the defense offered by Brown (1977):

> No one ever undertakes a philosophical analysis of science, or even a piece of scientific research, without a substantial body of prior commitments about how to proceed. If this generates a circle, it is not a vicious one since elements of the circle can be modified and the entire circle can be abandoned and replaced in the course of ongoing research.
>
> (p. 159)

Summary

The multiple hypotheses method is justified because it is the method by which science warrants claims to knowledge. In turn, science is justified because it appears to work well, and for good reasons. Science is based on sense data and the ability to sense the world has evolved over the eons to engender the species' survival. Science has been successful in enabling humans to better adapt to and alter the world. Although scientific knowledge is uncertain, science is self-correcting. And while human cognition remains limited and biased, scientific methods have evolved to cope with those limitations and biases. Science is the best means for understanding the world. And the MH method is the best means for conducting science.

Chapter 10

Conclusions

The hypothetico-deductive method focuses on a single hypothesis at a time. In contrast, the multiple hypotheses method explicitly addresses multiple hypotheses. The MH method not only involves testing a preferred hypothesis. It also involves evaluating alternative hypotheses. Therein resides its vast power as compared to the H-D method and to nonscientific approaches such as pseudoscience. Warranting a belief requires putting alternative beliefs into a survival-of-the-fittest competition where fitness is defined in terms of agreement with empirical evidence. The hypothetico-deductive method is often said to be the foundation of the scientific method. But, in fact, the multiple hypotheses method is the bedrock upon which science is founded. Indeed, the multiple hypotheses method is the ultimate method by which anyone (lawyers, doctors, auto mechanics, and the like) can reach justifiable and strong inferences about reality.

There is nothing esoteric about the multiple hypotheses method. It is just detailed and refined common sense. Once the logic of the MH method is understood, it is common sense to accept a hypothesis only after considering alternative hypotheses that might explain the same natural phenomenon. And it is only common sense to use extensive empirical data to choose among hypotheses about nature.

Unfortunately, researchers often teach their students the H-D method rather than the MH method. And most students learn the lesson all too well. "The fact is that most graduate students emerge with the notion that the only approved research is that in which a single hypothesis is tested by a single experiment" (Cattell, 1988, pp. 18). As a result, students overlook the benefits, and even the necessity, of examining multiple hypotheses. Strong inferences require strong research methods. The MH method is a strong research method.

Plausibility as the Criterion for Choosing among Hypotheses

A researcher cannot prove a hypothesis is correct. As noted in previous chapters, there will always be alternative hypotheses that can fit any pattern of data, at least in theory. As a result, it is not possible to decisively prove that only one of these hypotheses is correct. As also noted in previous chapters, it is also not

DOI: 10.4324/9781003198413-10

possible to disprove a hypothesis. Disproving a hypothesis requires showing that implications of the hypotheses do not hold true in the data. But deriving implications of a hypothesis always requires that auxiliary assumptions be made and, when data are not in agreement with the implications, it could be those auxiliary assumptions that are wrong rather than the hypothesis under question. Investigators also have to interpret the data they obtain and the interpretations they construct could be wrong. As a result, a definitive disproof of a hypothesis is out of reach. The best that can be done is to use the multiple hypotheses method to show that one hypothesis is plausible while alternative hypotheses are relatively implausible, given the data.

There are two important implications of using plausibility, rather than proof, as the criterion for choosing among hypotheses. First, without proof, the process of identifying potential hypotheses to explain evidence is never ending. At any given point in time, researchers tentatively choose to believe whichever available hypothesis is most plausible. However, if the set of available hypotheses does not contain the one that is correct, it obviously will not be possible to choose the correct hypothesis from among the set. To increase the chance that the correct hypothesis is available to be chosen, researchers have to continually try to identify new hypotheses, and resurrect old hypotheses, to add to the set from which hypotheses are chosen.

Second, researchers need to continually add new observations with which to choose among potential hypotheses. The available data determine which hypotheses are most plausible. However, it is possible that additional, new data would alter the relative plausibility of the available hypotheses. To increase the chance the correct hypothesis is chosen, researchers need to continually get more and more data so the plausibility of hypotheses can be assessed in the light of ever more complete information.

That the MH method demands diligence in collecting data is also justified from the perspective of pattern matching. As already noted in Chapter 3, the process of using data to choose among alternative hypotheses in the MH method is a process of pattern matching. Implications of a hypothesis predict a pattern in data. Implications are best derived so that different hypotheses predict different patterns. Then the task is to see which hypothesis best predicts the pattern that is evidenced. The more implications that are assessed, the more elaborate are the patterns and the easier it is to choose among hypotheses. That is, as the elaborateness of the pattern of observations increases, the plausibility of the hypothesis that well predicts the pattern tends to increase while the plausibility of alternative hypotheses that do not well predict the pattern tends to decrease. The way to rule out alternative hypotheses is

> by expanding as much as we can the number, range, and precision of confirmed predictions. The larger and more precise the set, the fewer will be the alternative explanations ....
>
> (Cook & Campbell, 1979, p. 22)

Such a strategy fits with the MH method's call for being diligent in obtaining data. Researchers should try to obtain as much evidence as possible and they should base their beliefs on the full complement of their evidence. Among other things, this means researchers should not base their beliefs on cherry picked evidence that favors only a preferred hypothesis.

Taken together, the need to continually identify hypotheses and to continually obtain data means the method of multiple hypotheses is conducted in a never-ending iterative cycle. Only in this way can researchers maximize the chances that their hypotheses about nature are correct. That researchers must be resigned to continue their work without end means they must also be resigned to never reach definitive answers. Researchers must forever stay open-minded—always willing to reevaluate their beliefs in the face of new data or the reinterpretations of old data. It is always possible that a new hypothesis will come along, or an old hypothesis will reappear, that better explains the available observations and which shows that the most cherished and trusted beliefs are no longer the most plausible. Researchers always need to be open to rethinking their understanding of the world. Nonetheless, it is rational to act and believe based on what is most plausible at any given time.

Both Expanding and Contracting the Number of Plausible Hypotheses

Identifying additional hypotheses and obtaining additional data are both expansive. That is, both adding more hypotheses and obtaining more data expand the scope of the investigation. But the process of obtaining more data, unlike the process of adding hypotheses, is performed in the service of contracting, rather than expanding, the number of plausible hypotheses. That is, the purpose of adding more data is to better choose among hypotheses so as to winnow out those hypotheses that are not as plausible as others. The two processes of expanding and winnowing are opposite but complementary. Popper (1965) talks of the process of expanding as involving conjecture while the process of winnowing involves refutation. Medawar (1996) describes the opposing processes as guesswork versus checkwork, and proposal versus disposal. Ayala (1994) characterizes the two tasks as discovery and confirmation:

> Scientific thinking may be characterized as a process of invention or discovery followed by validation or confirmation. One process concerns the formulation of new ideas ('acquisition of knowledge'), the other concerns their validation ('justification of knowledge').
>
> (p. 211)

The psychological skills required to perform the two complementary but opposite processes of enlarging the number of hypotheses and then narrowing them down are themselves complementary but opposite. In performing the task of identifying hypotheses, researchers need to be inventive and speculative. Researchers need to be open-minded and accepting. They need to think of how a hypothesis might be correct or at least plausible. In contrast, in performing the second task of winnowing down hypotheses, researchers need to be critical and skeptical. Researchers need to criticize each hypothesis—submit each hypothesis to sustained scrutiny. Researchers need to think of how a hypothesis might be incorrect and implausible. In this way, one of the tasks requires credulity while the other requires skepticism, where credulity and skepticism provide antagonistic perspectives.

To be able to do both tasks well, investigators must be able to switch perspectives depending on which task is at hand. For example, brainstorming is a well-accepted technique in problem solving whereby a participant is encouraged to come up with any and every possible idea no matter how crazy it might seem at the start. One of the rules in brainstorming is that the criticism of the ideas is not allowed at the beginning of the process, for criticism presumably stifles creativity. Only later, after the flow of novel ideas has slowed is a participant allowed to go back and prune away the unworkable ideas by criticizing them. But in criticizing, one of the apparently crazy ideas, that might not have emerged if the environment had been critical, might mutate into an idea that works well. The point is that credulity and skepticism are both necessary but at different times. You might never come up with the seeds of a brilliant idea if you are not a bit fanciful, unconstrained, and accepting. But you also would not be able to distinguish between brilliantly plausible and mundanely implausible hypotheses if, at some later point, you were not also critical.

Switching back and forth between credulity and skepticism is required for all innovative contributions. We must take imaginative risks (we must always go beyond the information given) but we must also be able to evaluate how well such risks work.

Science Is a Human Endeavor

That science requires both credulity and skepticism makes it a very human endeavor. That decisions must be based on plausibility rather than deductive proof also means science is a very human endeavor. Deciding what is most plausible is a personal judgment based, among other things, on a scientist's individual a priori beliefs and proclivities. That decisions are always tentative and subject to revision rather than certain and final, makes science fallible. Scientists need to be aware of the limitations and biases in their thinking so they can be taken into account in making reasoned judgments. The multiple hypotheses method does not replace reasoned judgment and common sense but rather depends on them in selecting among alternative hypotheses based on which is most plausible given the evidence. But at its best, the MH method also goes beyond common sense to provide the most rational means for deciding what to believe about reality.

The Scandal of Higher Education

Too much time is spent teaching students in higher education *what* to think and not enough time is spent teaching students *how* to think. Such a discrepancy is perhaps especially true in the sciences because science has learned so much about nature. As a result, textbooks in the sciences are usually chock full of research results about the workings of nature that students are expected to learn. But much less emphasis is placed on learning how to think scientifically, such as is involved in discovering interesting natural phenomena to explain, identifying alternative hypotheses to explain the phenomena, thinking of implications of the hypotheses, designing studies to assess the implications, interpreting the results of the studies, and drawing conclusions about which hypothesis or hypotheses to accept.

It is ironic that science education is not more focused on the methods of scientific investigations as compared to the results of scientific investigations. It is ironic because science offers the best methods for thinking about nature. At the very least, students should well understand the scientific method and be able to apply it. Yes, laboratory courses in the sciences provide practice in implementing the scientific method. But how well do students assimilate an understanding of the logic of the methods they are practicing? In my experience, most students cannot well articulate what the scientific method is. Students all too often are stymied when asked to explain how a hypothesis about nature can be justified. Students certainly do not have the identification and assessment of alternative hypotheses at the heart of whatever explanations they can provide. To my way of thinking, it is a scandal of higher education that academics do not spend more time teaching how to think as compared to what to think. Scientists in academe should spend more time explicitly teaching the MH method as the best means for how to think when attempting to understand nature.

The Primacy of Alternatives

So far, I have emphasized the use of the MH method in science. But the lessons the MH method teaches can be used in all inquiry, and not just in scientific inquiry into nature. The heart of the MH method is identifying and assessing alternatives. If reduced to just two words, the essence of the MH method is to consider alternatives. The value of considering alternatives applies quite generally. Consider alternatives when interpreting literature, designing architecture, developing philosophical arguments, appreciating art, making a film, managing a business, playing sports, voting for political candidates, making decisions in everyday life (including decisions about finances, health, nutrition, and interacting with others), and so on. It is wise to consider alternatives in both science and other endeavors to engage with the world. Writ large that is what the method of multiple hypotheses teaches.

References

Adams, K. A., & Lawrence, E. K. (2019). *Research methods, statistics, and applications* (2nd ed.). Thousand Oaks, CA: Sage.

American Psychological Association (2020). *Publication Manual of the American Psychological Association* (7th ed.), Washington, D.C.: American Psychological Association.

Ayala, F. J. (1994). On the scientific method, its practice and pitfalls. *History and Philosophy of the Life Sciences*, 16(2), 205–240.

Bauer, H. H. (1992). *Scientific literacy and the myth of the scientific method.* Urbana, IL: University of Illinois Press.

Birnbaum, P. (January 24, 2011). "Scorecasting": Is home field advantage just biased officiating? Sabermetric Research. http://blog.philbirnbaum.com/2011/01/scorecasting-is-home-field-advantage.html.

Brand, M. (Ed.). (1976). *The nature of causation.* Urbana, IL: University of Illinois Press.

Brand, M. (1979). Causality. In P. D. Asquith & H. E. Kyburg, Jr. (Eds.), *Current research in philosophy of science.* East Lansing, MI: Philosophy of Science Association.

Bridgeman, P. W. (1955). *Reflections of a physicist.* New York, NY: Philosophical Library.

Bronowski, J. (1978). *The common sense of science.* Cambridge, MA: Harvard University Press.

Brook, S. L. (2012). Book review. *Journal of Sports Economics*, 24(2), 218–220.

Brown, H. I. (1977). *Perception, theory and commitment: The new philosophy of science.* Chicago, IL: University of Chicago Press.

Campbell, D. T. (1957). Factors relevant to the validity of experiments in social settings. *Psychological Bulletin*, 54(4), 297–312.

Campbell, D. T. (1966). Pattern matching as an essential in distal knowing. In K. R. Hammond (Ed.), *The psychology of Egon Brunswik* (pp. 81–106). New York: Holt, Rinehart & Winston.

Campbell, D. T. (1969). Reforms as experiments. *American Psychologist*, 24(4), 409–429.

Campbell, D. T. (1970). Legal reforms as experiments. *Journal of Legal Education*, 23(1), 217–239.

Campbell, D. T. (1972). Measuring the effects of social innovations by means of time-series. In J. M. Tanur, F. Mosteller, W. H. Kruskal, R. F. Link, R. S. Pieters, & G. R. Rising (Eds.), *Statistics: A guide to the unknown* (pp. 120–129). San Francisco, CA: Holden-Day.

Campbell, D. T. (1974). Unjustified variation and selective retention in scientific discovery. In F. J. Ayala & T. Dobzhansky (Eds.), *Studies in the philosophy of biology* (pp. 140–161). New York, NY: Macmillan.

Campbell, D. T. (1984). Can we be scientific in applied science? In R. F. Connor, D. G. Altman, & C. Jackson (Eds.), *Evaluation studies review annual* (Vol. 9, pp. 26–48). Newbury Park, CA: Sage.

Campbell, D. T. (1988a). A phenomenology of the other one: Corrigible, hypothetical, and critical. In E. S. Overman (Ed.), *Methodology and epistemology for social science: Selected papers* (pp. 337–359). Chicago, IL: University of Chicago Press. Originally published as Campbell, D. T. (1969). A phenomenology of the other one: Corrigible, hypothetical, and critical. In T. Mischel (Ed.), *Human action: Conceptual and empirical issues* (pp. 41–69). New York, NY: Academic Press.

Campbell, D. T. (1988b). Descriptive epistemology: Psychological, sociological, and evolutionary. In E. S. Overman (Ed.), *Methodology and epistemology for social science: Selected papers* (pp. 435–486). Chicago, IL: University of Chicago Press. Originally published as Campbell, D. T. (1977). *Descriptive epistemology: Psychological, sociological, and evolutionary*. Cambridge, MA: Harvard University Press.

Campbell, D. T. (1988c). Evolutional epistemology. In E. S. Overman (Ed.), *Methodology and epistemology for social science: Selected papers* (pp. 393–434). Chicago, IL: University of Chicago Press. Originally published as Campbell, D. T. (1974). Evolutionary epistemology. In P. A. Schilpp (Ed.), *The philosophy of Karl Popper* (Vol. 14 of The Library of Living Philosophers, pp. 413–463). La Salle, IL: Open Court Publishing.

Campbell, D. T. (1988d). Prospective: Artifact and control. In E. S. Overman (Ed.), *Methodology and epistemology for social science: Selected papers* (pp. 167–190). Chicago, IL: University of Chicago Press. Originally published as Campbell, D. T. (1969). Prospective: Artifact and control. In R. Rosenthal, & R. Rosnow (Eds.), *Artifact in behavior Research* (pp. 351–382). New York, NY: Academic Press.

Campbell, D. T. (1988e). Qualitative knowing in action research. In E. S. Overman (Ed.), *Methodology and epistemology for social science: Selected papers* (pp. 360–376). Chicago, IL: University of Chicago Press. Originally published as Campbell, D. T. (1978). Qualitative knowing in action research. In M. Brenner, P. Marsh, & M. Brenner (Eds.), *The social contexts of method* (pp. 184–209). Beckenham, UK: Croom Helm.

Campbell, D. T. (1988f). Science's social system of validity-enhancing collective belief change and the problems of the social sciences. In E. S. Overman (Ed.), *Methodology and epistemology for social science: Selected papers* (pp. 504–523). Chicago, IL: University of Chicago Press. Originally published as Campbell, D. T. (1986). Science's social system of validity-enhancing collective belief change and the problems of the social sciences. In D. W. Fiske, & R. A. Shweder (Eds.), *Metatheory in social science: Pluralisms and subjectivities* (pp. 108–135). Chicago, IL: University of Chicago Press.

Campbell, D. T., & Ross, H. L. (1968). The Connecticut crackdown on speeding: Time-series data in quasi-experimental analysis. *Law and Society Review*, 3(1), 33–53.

Campbell, D. T., & Stanley, J. C. (1966). *Experimental and quasi-experimental designs for research*. Skokie, IL: Rand McNally.

Carey, S. S. (2004). *A beginner's guide to scientific method* (3rd ed.). Belmont, CA: Wadsworth.

Cattell, R. B. (1988). Psychological theory and scientific method. In J. R. Nesselroade & R. B. Cattell (Eds.), *Handbook of multivariate experimental psychology* (2nd ed., pp. 3–20). New York: Plenum Press.

Chalmers, A. (2013). *What is this thing called science?* (4th ed.). Indianapolis, IN: Hackett Publishing.

Chamberlin, T. C. (1890/1965). The method of multiple working hypotheses. *Science* (New Series), 148(3671), 754–759.

Cochran, W. G. (1965). The planning of observational studies of human populations (with discussion). *Journal of the Royal Statistical Society* (Series A), 128(2), 234–266.

Cook, T. D. (1985). Post-positivist critical multiplism. In R. L. Shotland & M. M. Mark (Eds.), *Social science and social policy* (pp. 21–62). Beverly Hills, CA: Sage.

Cook, T. D., & Campbell, D. T. (1979). *Quasi-experimentation: Design and analysis issues for field settings*. Skokie, IL: Rand McNally.

Coon, D., & Mitterer, J. O. (2016). *Introduction to psychology: Gateway to mind and behavior* (14th ed.). Boston, MA: Cengage.

Copi, I. M. (1978). *Introduction to logic* (5th ed.). New York, NY: Macmillan.

Dawkins, R. (2009). *The greatest show on earth: The evidence for evolution*. New York, NY: Free Press.

Dewey, J. (1966). *Democracy and education*. New York, NY: Free Press.

Dobzhansky, T. (1973). Nothing in biology makes sense except in the light of evolution. *American Biology Teacher*, 35(3), 125–129.

Donohue, J. J., III, & Levitt, S. D. (2001). The impact of legalized abortion on crime. *The Quarterly Journal of Economics*, 116(2), 379–420.

Donohue, J. J., & Levitt, S. (2020). The impact of legalized abortion on crime over the last two decades. *American Law and Economics Review*, 22(2), 241–302.

Duhem, P. (1906, tr. 1962). *The aim and structure of physical theory*. New York, NY: Athenum.

Einstein, A. (1922). *Sidelights on Relativity*. Translated by G.B. Jeffry & W. Perrett, www.ibiblio.org/ebooks/Einstein/Sidelights/Einstein_Sidelights.pdf.

Einstein, A. (2003). Physics and reality. *Daedalus*, 132(4), 22–25.

Ennis, R. H. (1987). A taxonomy of critical thinking dispositions and abilities. In J. Baron and R. Sternberg (Eds.), *Teaching thinking skills: Theory and practice* (pp. 9–26). New York, NY: Freeman.

Feldman, R. S. (2011). *Understanding psychology* (10th ed.). New York, NY: McGraw-Hill.

Feyerabend, P. (1975). *Against method*. London: Verso.

Feynman, R. P. (1965). *The character of physical law*. Cambridge, MA: MIT Press.

Feynman, R. P. (1998). *The meaning of it all: Thoughts of a citizen-scientist*. Reading, MA: Perseus Books.

Foote, C. L., & Goetz, C. F. (2008). The impact of legalized abortion on crime: A comment. *The Quarterly Journal of Economics*, 123(1), 407–423.

Frank, P. G. (1956). The variety of reasons for the acceptance of scientific theories. In P. G. Frank (Ed.). *The validation of scientific theories* (pp. 3–18). Boston, MA: The Beacon Press.

Furby, L. (1973). Interpreting regression toward the mean in developmental research. *Developmental Psychology*, 8(2), 172–179.

Garrison, J. W. (1986). Some principles of postpositivistic philosophy of science. *Educational Researcher*, 15(9), 12–18.

Giddens, A., Duneier, M., Applebaum, R. P., & Carr, D. (2016). *Introduction to sociology* (10th ed.). New York, NY: W.W. Norton.

Giere, R. (1998). Justifying scientific theories. In E. D. Klemke, R. Hollinger, & D. W. Rudge, with D. A. Kline (Eds.) *Introductory readings in the philosophy of science* (pp. 415–434). Amherst, NY: Prometheus Books. From Giere, R. (Ed.) (1984). *Justifying scientific theories: Understanding scientific reasoning* (2nd ed.). New York, NY: Holt, Rinehart & Winston.

Godfrey-Smith, P. (2003). *Theory and reality: An introduction to the philosophy of science*. Chicago, IL: University of Chicago Press.

Goldstein, M., & Goldstein. I. (1984). *The experience of science: An interdisciplinary approach*. New York, NY: Plenum.
Gorham, G. (2009). *Philosophy of science: A beginner's guide*. Oxford: Oneworld Publications.
Greenwald, A. G., Pratkanis, A. R., Leippe, M. R., & Baumgardner, M. H. (1986). Under what conditions does theory obstruct research progress? *Psychological Review*, 93 (2), 216–229.
Grison, S., Heatherton, T. F., & Gazzaniga, M. S. (2017). *Psychology in your life* (2nd ed.). New York, NY: W.W. Norton.
Hall, H. (2006). Teaching pigs to sing: An experiment in bringing critical thinking to the masses. *Skeptical Inquirer*, 30, 36–39.
Hall, R. J., & Johnson, C. R. (1998). The epistemic duty to seek more evidence. *American Philosophical Quarterly*, 35(2), 129–139.
Hanson, N. R. (1958). *Patterns of discovery: An inquiry into the conceptual foundations of science*. Cambridge: Cambridge University Press.
Harman, G. H. (1965). The inference to the best explanation. *The Philosophical Review*, 74(1), 88–95.
Hempel, C. G. (1952). Some theses on empirical certainty. *The Review of Metaphysics*, 5 (4), 621–622.
Hempel, C. G. (1966). *Philosophy of natural science*. Englewood Cliffs, NJ: Prentice-Hall.
Hines, T. (2003). *Pseudoscience and the paranormal* (2nd ed.). Buffalo, NY: Prometheus.
Hume, D. (1778). *A treatise of human nature*. L. A. Selby-Bigge (Ed.) (2nd ed.). Oxford: Oxford University Press.
Johnson, R. B., Russo, F., & Schoonenboom, J. (2019). Causation in mixed methods research: The meeting of philosophy, science, and practice. *Journal of Mixed Methods Research*, 13(2), 143–162.
Josephson, J. R. (1994). Conceptual analysis of abduction. In J. R. Josephson, & S. G. Josephson (Eds.), *Abductive inference: Computation, philosophy, technology* (pp. 5–30). Cambridge: Cambridge University Press.
Josephson, J. R., & Josephson, S. G. (Eds.). (1994). *Abductive inference: Computation, philosophy, technology*. Cambridge: Cambridge University Press.
Kaplan, A. (1964). *The conduct of inquiry: Methodology for behavioral science*. New York, NY: Chandler Publishing.
Kean, S. (2012). *The violinist's thumb: And other lost tales of love, war, and genius, as written by our genetic code*. New York, NY: Little Brown.
Kidd, R. F. (1976). Manipulation checks: Advantage or disadvantage? *Representative Research in Social Psychology*, 7(2), 160–165.
Kitcher, P. (1995). *The advancement of science*. Oxford: Oxford University Press.
Klee, R. (1997). *Introduction to the philosophy of science: Cutting nature at its seams*. Oxford: Oxford University Press.
Krathwohl, D. R. (1985). *Social and behavioral science research*. San Francisco, CA: Jossey-Bass.
Kuhn, T. S. (1970). *The structure of scientific revolutions* (2nd ed., enlarged). Chicago, IL: University of Chicago Press.
Kuhn, T. S. (1998). Objectivity, value judgment, and theory choice. In E. D. Klemke, R. Hollinger, & D. W. Rudge with A. D. Kline (Eds.), *Introductory readings in the philosophy of science* (pp. 435–450). Amherst, NY: Prometheus Books. From Kuhn, T. S. (1977). *Essential tension* (pp. 320–339). Chicago, IL: University of Chicago Press.

Ladyman, J. (2002). *Understanding philosophy of science*. London: Routledge.

Lakatos, I. (1968). Criticism and the methodology of scientific research programmes. *Proceedings of the Aristotelian Society*, 69(1), 149–186.

Lakatos, I. (1970). Falsification and the methodology of scientific research programmes. In I. Lakatos & A. Musgrave (Eds.) *Criticism and the growth of knowledge* (pp. 91–196). Cambridge: Cambridge University Press.

Lakatos, I. (1978). *The methodology of scientific research programmes: Philosophical papers* (Vol. 1). Cambridge: Cambridge University Press.

Laudan, L. (1998a). Commentary: Science at the bar—causes for concern. In M. Curd, & J. A. Cover (Eds.), *Philosophy of science: The central issues* (pp. 48–53). New York, NY: W. W. Norton. From Laudan, L. (1982). *Science, Technology, and Human Values*, 7(41), 16–19.

Laudan, L. (1998b). Demystifying underdetermination. In M. Curd, & J. A. Cover (Eds.), *Philosophy of science: The central issues* (pp. 320–353). New York, NY: W. W. Norton. From C. W. Savage (Ed.). (1990). *Scientific theories. Minnesota studies in the philosophy of science* (Vol. 14, pp. 267–297). Minneapolis, MN: University of Minnesota Press.

Levitt, S. D. (2004). Understanding why crime fell in the 1990s: Four factors that explain the decline and six that do not. *Journal of Economic Perspective*, 18(1), 163–190.

Levitt, S. D., & Dubner, S. J. (2005). *Freakonomics: A rogue economist explores the hidden side of everything*. New York, NY: William Morrow.

Lilienfeld, S. O., Lohr, J. M., & Morier, D. (2001). The teaching of courses in the science and pseudoscience of psychology: Useful resources. *Teaching of Psychology*, 28(3), 182–191.

Lipton, P. (2004). *Inference to the best explanation* (2nd ed.). London: Routledge.

Lord, C., Ross, L., & Lepper, M., (1979). Biased assimilation and attitude polarization: The effects of prior theories on subsequently considered evidence. *Journal of Personality and Social Psychology*, 37(11), 2098–2109.

Lorenz, K. (1941). Kants lehre vom apriorishen im lichte gegenwartiger biologie. *Blätter für Deutsche Philosophie*, 15, 94–125. Translated in L. von Bertalanffy & A. Rapoport (Eds.) (1962), *General systems* (Vol. 7, pp. 23–35). Ann Arbor, MI: Society for General Systems Research.

Lott, J. R., & Whitley, J. E., (2007). Abortion and crime: Unwanted children and out-of-wedlock births. *Economic Inquiry*, 45(2), 304–324.

Marder, M. P. (2011). *Research methods for science*. Cambridge: Cambridge University Press.

Mcauliffe, W. H. B. (2015). How did abduction get confused with inference to the best explanation? *Transactions of the Charles S. Peirce Society: A Quarterly Journal in American Philosophy*, 51(3), 300–319.

Medawar, P. (1996). *The strange case of the spotted mice and other classic essays on science*. Oxford: Oxford University Press.

Meehl, P. E. (1978). Theoretical risks and tabular asterisks: Sir Karl, Sir Ronald, and the slow progress in soft psychology. *Journal of Consulting and Clinical Psychology*, 46(4), 806–834.

Miles, M. B., & Huberman, A. M. (1994). *Qualitative data analysis: An expanded sourcebook*. Thousand Oaks, CA: Sage.

Moskowitz, T. J., & Wertheim, L. J. (2011). *Scorecasting: The hidden influences behind how sports are played and games are won*. New York, NY: Crown Archetype.

Newton-Smith, W. H. (1981). *The rationality of science*. Boston, MA: Routledge & Kegan Paul.

Nisbett, R., & Ross, L. (1980). *Human inference: Strategies and shortcomings of social judgment.* Englewood Cliffs, NJ: Prentice-Hall.

Okasha, S. (2016). *Philosophy of science: A very short introduction.* Oxford: Oxford University Press.

OpenStax. (2019). *Introduction to sociology* (2nd ed.). https://cnx.org/contents/AgQDEnLI@13.6:TrIRM88K@9/Introduction-to-Sociology.

Phillips, D. C. (1987a). The new logic of science. In D. C. Phillips (Ed.), *Philosophy, science, and social inquiry: Contemporary methodological controversies in social science and related applied fields of research* (pp. 5–19). Oxford: Pergamon Press.

Phillips, D. C. (1987b). The new philosophy of science run rampant. In D. C. Phillips (Ed.), *Philosophy, science, and social inquiry: Contemporary methodological controversies in social science and related applied fields of research.* (pp. 80–101). Oxford: Pergamon Press.

Phillips, D. C. (1992a). New philosophy of science. In D. C. Phillips (Ed.), *The social scientist's bestiary: A guild to fabled threats to, and defenses of, naturalistic social science* (pp. 50–62). Oxford: Pergamon Press. Originally published as Phillips, D. C. (1990). Postpositivistic science: Myths and realities. In E. Guba (Ed.), *The paradigm debate* (pp. 31–45). Newbury Park, CA: Sage.

Phillips, D. C. (1992b). Qualitative research and its warrant. In D. C. Phillips (Ed.), *The social scientist's bestiary: A guild to fabled threats to, and defenses of, naturalistic social science* (pp. 106–119). Oxford: Pergamon Press. Originally published as Phillips, D. C. (1987). Validity in qualitative research: Why the worry about warrant will not wane. *Education and Urban Society*, 20(1), 9–24.

Phillips, D. C. (1992c). The hermeneutics and naturalistic social inquiry. In D. C. Phillips (Ed.), *The social scientist's bestiary: A guild to fabled threats to, and defenses of, naturalistic social science* (pp. 1–20). Oxford:Pergamon Press. Originally published as Phillips, D. C. (1991) Hermeneutics: A threat to scientific social science? *International Journal of Educational Research*, 15(6), 553–568.

Pierce, C. S. (1931). Notes of scientific philosophy. In C. Hartshorne, and P. Weiss (Eds.), *Collected papers of Charles Sanders Pierce* (Vol. 1). Cambridge MA: Harvard University Press. [Original manuscript 1897.]

Pirsig, R. M. (1999). *Zen and the art of motorcycle maintenance: An inquiry into values.* New York, NY: William Morrow.

Platt, J. R. (1964). Strong inference. *Science*, 146(3642), 347–353.

Popper, K. R. (1965). *Conjectures and refutations: The growth of scientific knowledge.* New York, NY: Harper Torchbooks.

Popper, K. R. (1968). *The logic of scientific discovery.* New York, NY: Harper Torchbooks.

Popper, K. R. (1972). *Objective knowledge.* Oxford: Oxford University Press.

Potochnik, A., Colombo, M., & Wright, C. (2019). *Recipes for science: An introduction to scientific methods and reasoning.* New York: Routledge.

Privitera, G. J., & Ahlgrim-Delzell, L. (2019). *Research methods for education.* Thousand Oaks, CA: Sage.

Quine, W. V. O. (1951). Two dogmas of empiricism. *The Philosophical Review*, 60(1), 20–43.

Quine, W. V. O. (1961). *From a logical point of view* (2nd ed.). New York NY: Harper Torchbooks.

Reichardt, C. S. (2019). *Quasi-experimentation: A guide to design and analysis.* New York, NY: Guilford Publications.

Rosenberg, A. (2012). *Philosophy of science: A contemporary introduction* (3rd ed.). New York: Routledge.

Ruscio, J. (2006). *Clear thinking with psychology: Separating sense from nonsense* (2nd ed.). Belmont, CA: Thomson Wadsworth.

Russell, B. (1931). *The scientific outlook.* New York, NY: W.W. Norton.

Sagan, C. (1979). *Broca's brain: Reflections on the romance of science.* New York, NY: Random House.

Sagan, C. (1991). The burden of skepticism. In K. Frazier (Ed.), *The hundredth monkey and other paradigms of the paranormal* (pp. 1–9). Amherst, NY: Prometheus Books.

Sagan, C. (1995). *The demon-haunted world: Science as a candle in the dark.* New York, NY: Random House.

Salmon, W. C. (1998). Rationality and objectivity in science or Tom Kuhn meets Tom Bayes. In M. Curd, & J. A. Cover (Eds.), *Philosophy of science: The central issues.* New York, NY: W. W. Norton (pp. 551–583). From C. W. Savage (Ed.). (1990). *Scientific theories* (Vol. 14). Minnesota studies in the philosophy of science (pp. 175–204). Minneapolis, MN: University of Minnesota Press.

Shadish, W. R. (1993). Critical multiplism: A research strategy and its attendant tactics. In L. B. Sechrest & A. J. Figueredo (Eds.), *New directions for evaluation* (Vol. 60, pp. 13–57). San Francisco, CA: Jossey-Bass.

Shadish, W. R., Cook, T. D., & Campbell, D. T. (2002). *Experimental and quasi-experimental designs for generalized causal inference.* Boston, MA: Houghton Mifflin.

Simons, D. J., & Chabris, C. F. (1999). Gorillas in our midst: Sustained inattentional blindness by dynamic events. *Perception*, 28(9), 1059–1074.

Staley, K. W. (2014). *An introduction to the philosophy of science.* Cambridge: Cambridge University Press.

Stanovich, K. E. (2004). *How to think straight about psychology* (7th ed.). Boston, MA: Allyn & Bacon.

Thagard, P. R. (1998). Why astrology is a pseudoscience. In M. Curd, & J. A. Cover (Eds.), *Philosophy of science: The central issues* (pp. 27–37). New York, NY: W. W. Norton. From Thagard, P. R. (1978). Why astrology is a pseudoscience. In P. Asquith & I. Hacking (Eds.), *Proceedings of the Philosophy of Science Association* (Vol. 1, pp. 223–234). East Lansing, MI: Philosophy of Science Association.

Toulmin, S. E. (1961). *Foresight and understanding: An inquiry into the aims of science.* Bloomington, IN: Indiana University Press.

Trochim, W. M. K. (1985). Pattern matching, validity, and conceptualization in program evaluation. *Evaluation Review*, 9(5), 575–604.

Tversky, A., & Kahneman, D. (1982). Judgment under uncertainty: Heuristics and biases. In D. Kahneman, P. Slovic, & A. Tversky (Eds.), *Judgment under uncertainty: Heuristics and biases* (pp. 3–20). Cambridge: Cambridge University Press. Reprinted from Tversky, A. & Kahneman, D. (1974). Judgment under uncertainty: Heuristics and biases. *Science*, 185(4157), 1124–1131.

Van Fraassen, B. C. (1980). *The scientific image.* Oxford: Clarendon Press.

Walton, D. (2005). *Abductive reasoning.* Tuscaloosa, AL: University of Alabama Press.

Weaver, W. (1967). *Science and imagination: Selected papers.* New York, NY: Basic Books.

Weiten, W. (2013). *Psychology: Themes and variations* (9th ed.). Belmont, CA: Wadsworth.

Wimsatt, W. C. (1981). Robustness, reliability, and overdetermination. In M. B. Brewer & B. E. Collins (Eds.), *Scientific inquiry and the social sciences: A volume in honor of Donald T. Campbell* (pp. 124–163). San Francisco, CA: Jossey-Bass.

Index

Page numbers in italics refer to figures.

For Product Safety Concerns and Information please contact our EU
representative GPSR@taylorandfrancis.com
Taylor & Francis Verlag GmbH, Kaufingerstraße 24, 80331 München, Germany

www.ingramcontent.com/pod-product-compliance
Ingram Content Group UK Ltd.
Pitfield, Milton Keynes, MK11 3LW, UK
UKHW021723240926
475702UK00030BA/2387
9781032054605